AFRICAN
FASHIONS

By Diana Murray

Get to know the artist and shop for unique printable coloring pages at:

ColorByCulture.com

THIS COLORING BOOK BELONGS TO:

_____

DATE:

_____

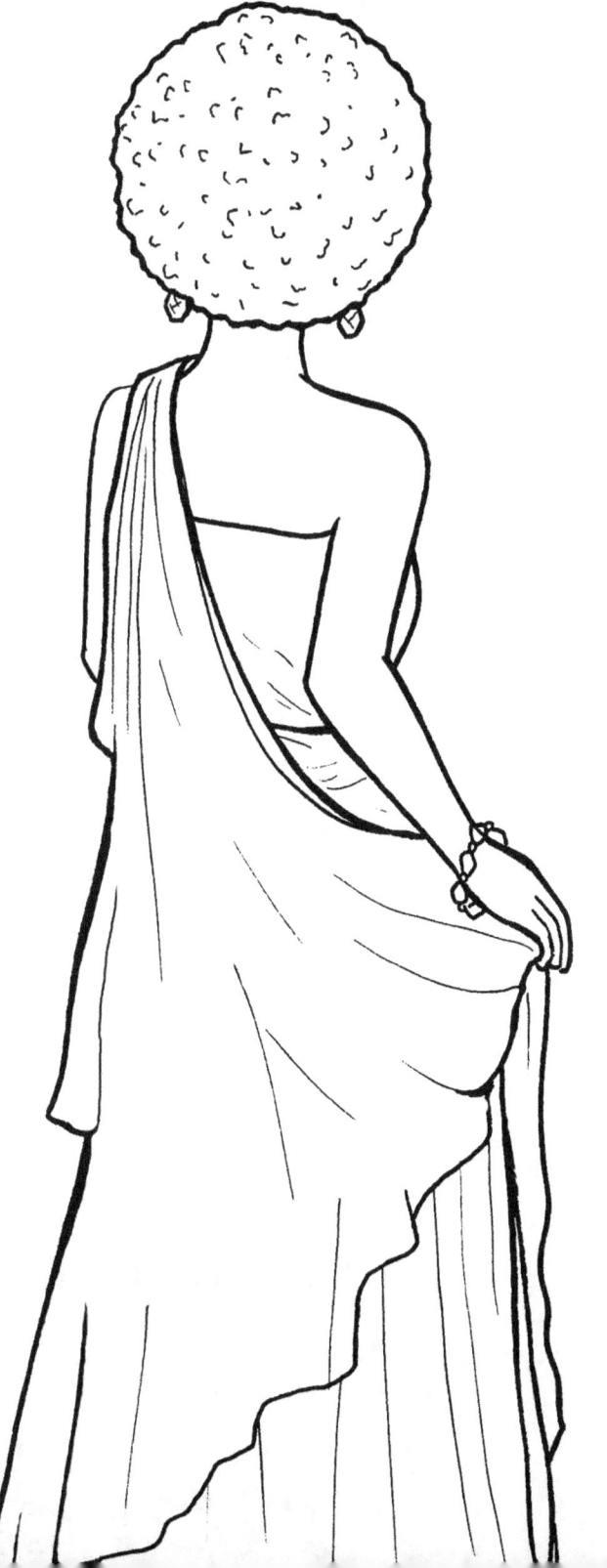

COLORING THIS BOOK

Did you know that Africa is the second largest continent in the world? It's also home to 54 countries and thousands of people groups. It is nearly impossible to capture all the beauty that Africa has to offer, but this book is my first step in trying!

The fashions in this book are inspired by traditional and modern styles that are worn by women across the continent. I hope you enjoy coloring the many bold patterns and intricate accessories that are a hallmark of African adornment. Included in this collection are 24 beautiful women representing 12 different African countries. You'll also find 6 bonus pages featuring modern African trends, some of which you can add your own designs and patterns to!

The best tools for coloring these pages are colored pencils, which allow you to easily fill in the smaller details. I recommend placing a sheet of card stock behind the page you are working on or carefully cutting out the page before coloring. This way you can avoid indentations on the following pages.

You may also make photocopies for your own personal use. By copying these images onto paper or card stock you will be able to use other artist tools such as markers without the color bleeding through or warping the paper.

Your creativity is what will make this book unique! Please feel free to use these images in book reviews and to share your colored pages on social media outlets such as Instagram, Pinterest, and Facebook. Use **#colorbyculture** for a chance to be featured on my Instagram account (@colorbyculture).

As you color these pages, the most important thing to remember is to have fun. So find a cozy spot, grab your art supplies, and let your journey to Africa begin!

Happy Coloring,

Diana Murray

THE ILLUSTRATIONS

African Fashions has 24 illustrations that represent 12 different countries. The next few pages will let you know where these styles are worn throughout Africa. Some clothing is specific to a certain country or ethnic group, while others are modern styles that are also worn in many other African countries.

From left to right:

1. Chad, traditional dress

2. Chad, Wodaabe woman

3. Nigeria, modern dress

4. Nigeria, modern dress

5. Kenya, Maasai woman

6. Kenya, modern dress

7. Gabon, traditional bridal dress

8. Gabon, modern dress

9. Somalia, traditional dress

10. Somalia, modern dress

11. Malawi, traditional dress

12. Malawi, modern dress

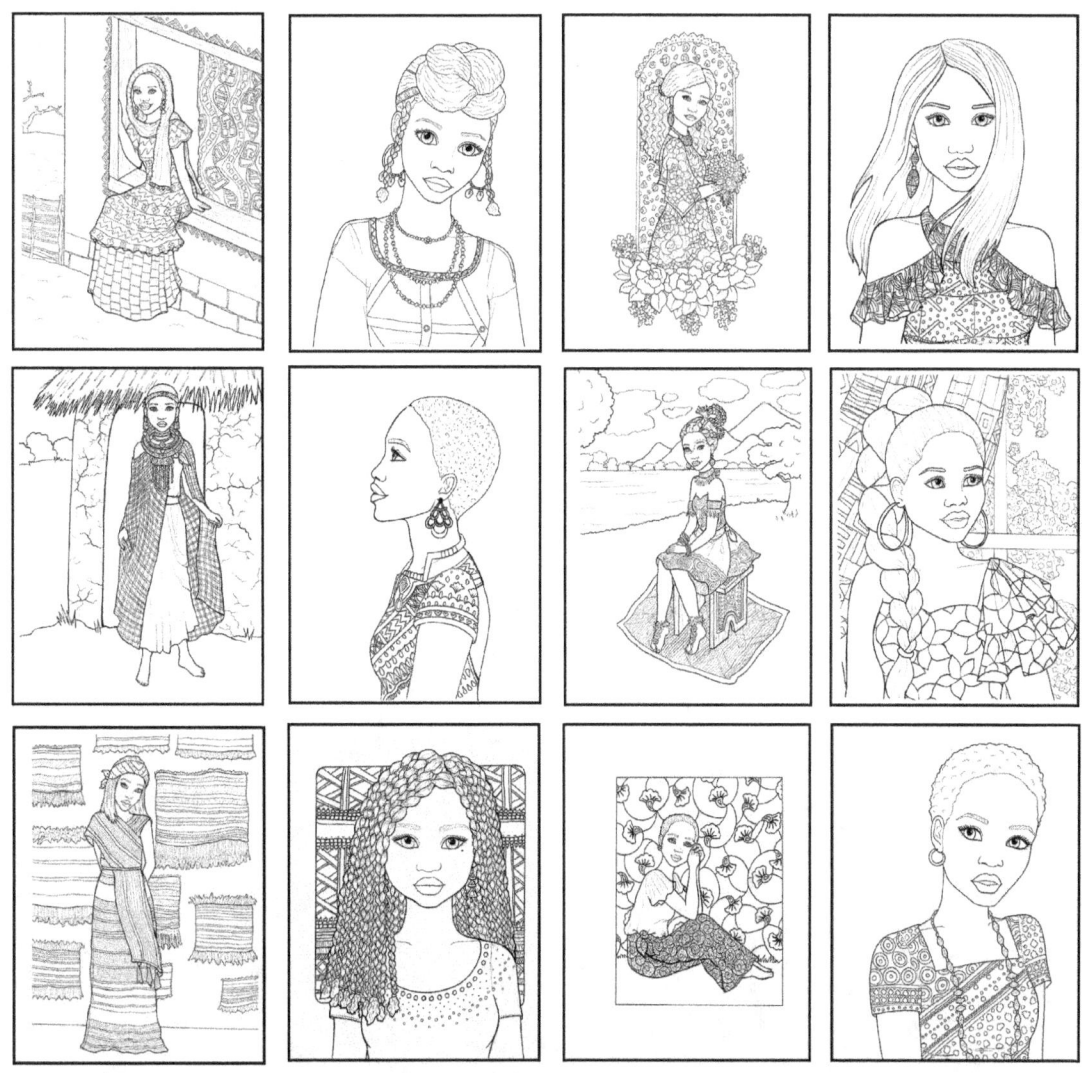

THE ILLUSTRATIONS

If you want your coloring to be culturally realistic, try using Pinterest or Google Images to search for pictures from that country or ethnicity. In many cases, all kinds of colors are used in African clothing. But for certain ethnic groups, you may see colors that are more common than others.

1. Morocco, traditional bridal dress

2. Morocco, Berber woman

3. Ghana, Krobo woman

4. Ghana, traditional dress

5. Senegal, modern dress

6. Senegal, traditional dress

7. Liberia, traditional dress

8. Liberia, modern dress

9. Eritrea, traditional dress

10. Eritrea, Hedarab woman

11. Rwanda, traditional dress

12. Rwanda, traditional dress

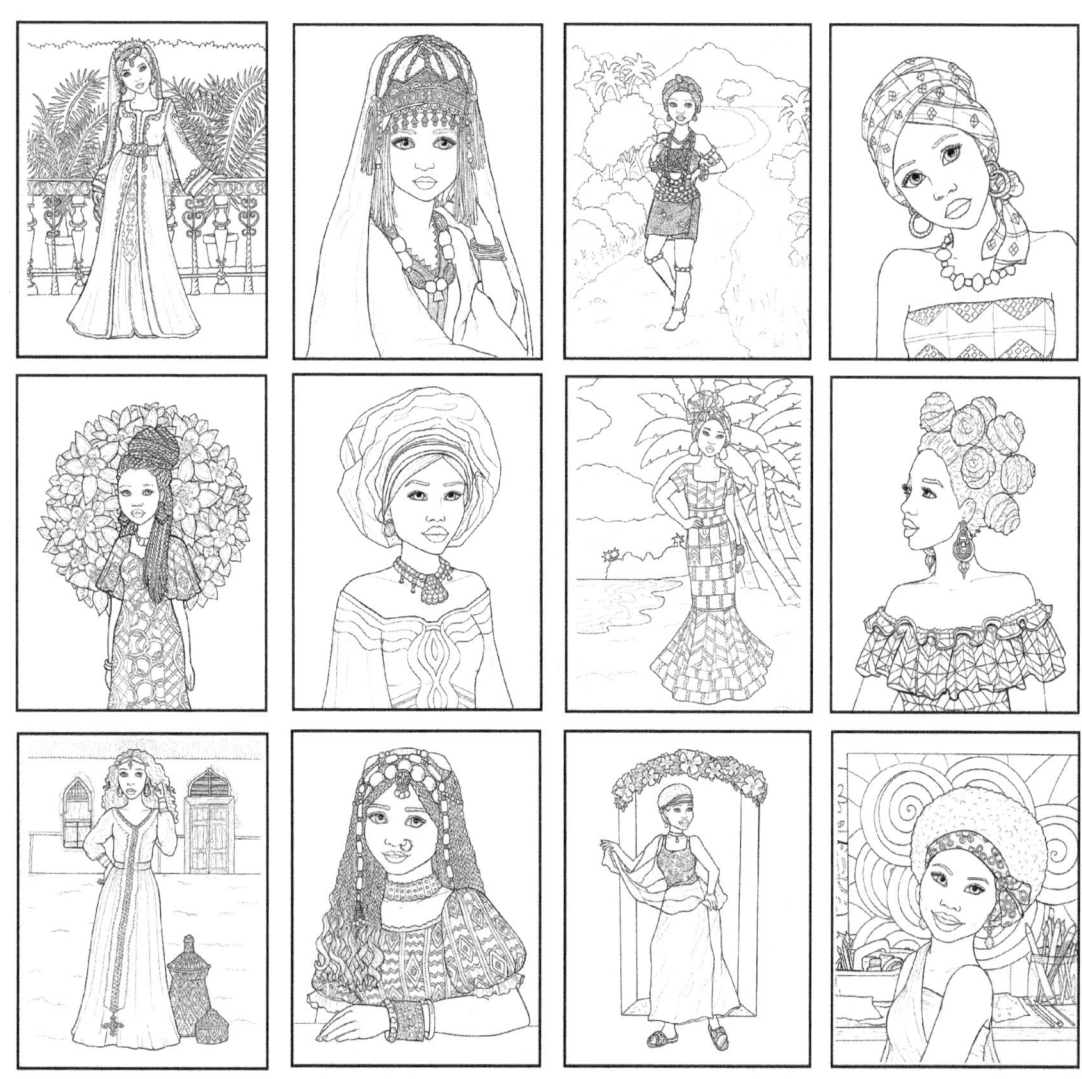

BONUS FASHION PAGES

The last 6 pages in this book feature modern African fashions and hairstyles. You can have fun designing and coloring your own patterns on the first 3 pages, and you can get creative with hair and make-up on last 3 pages.

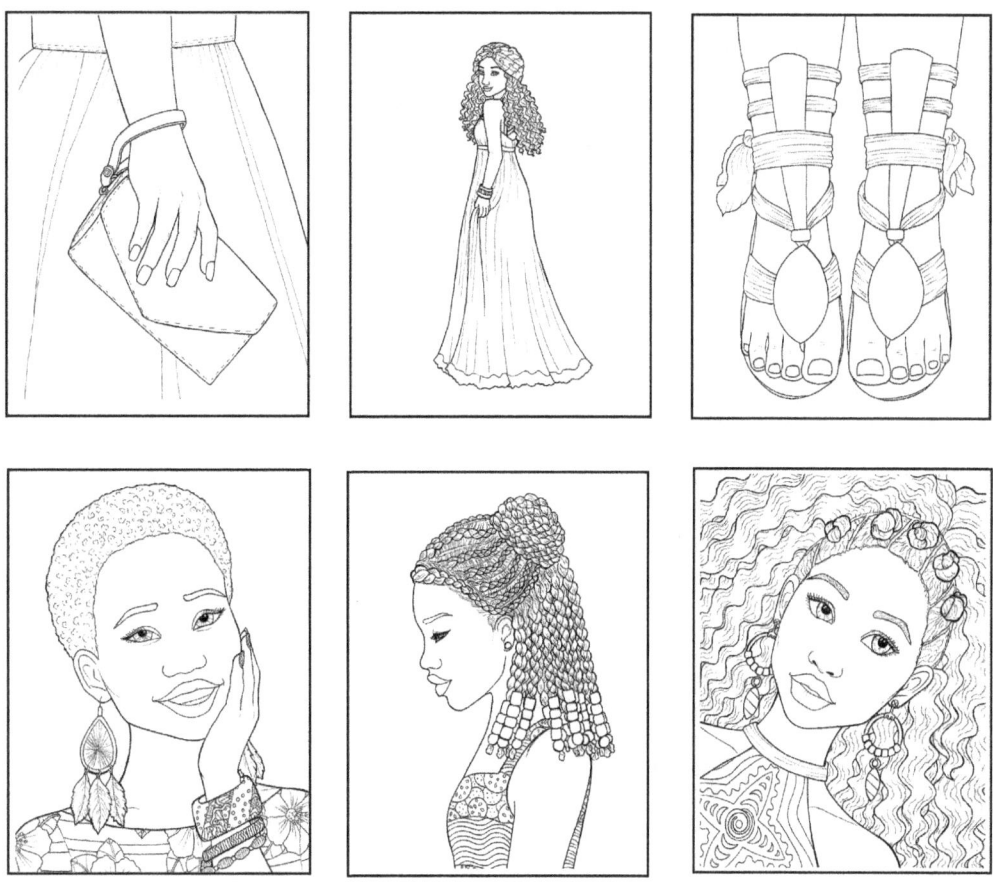

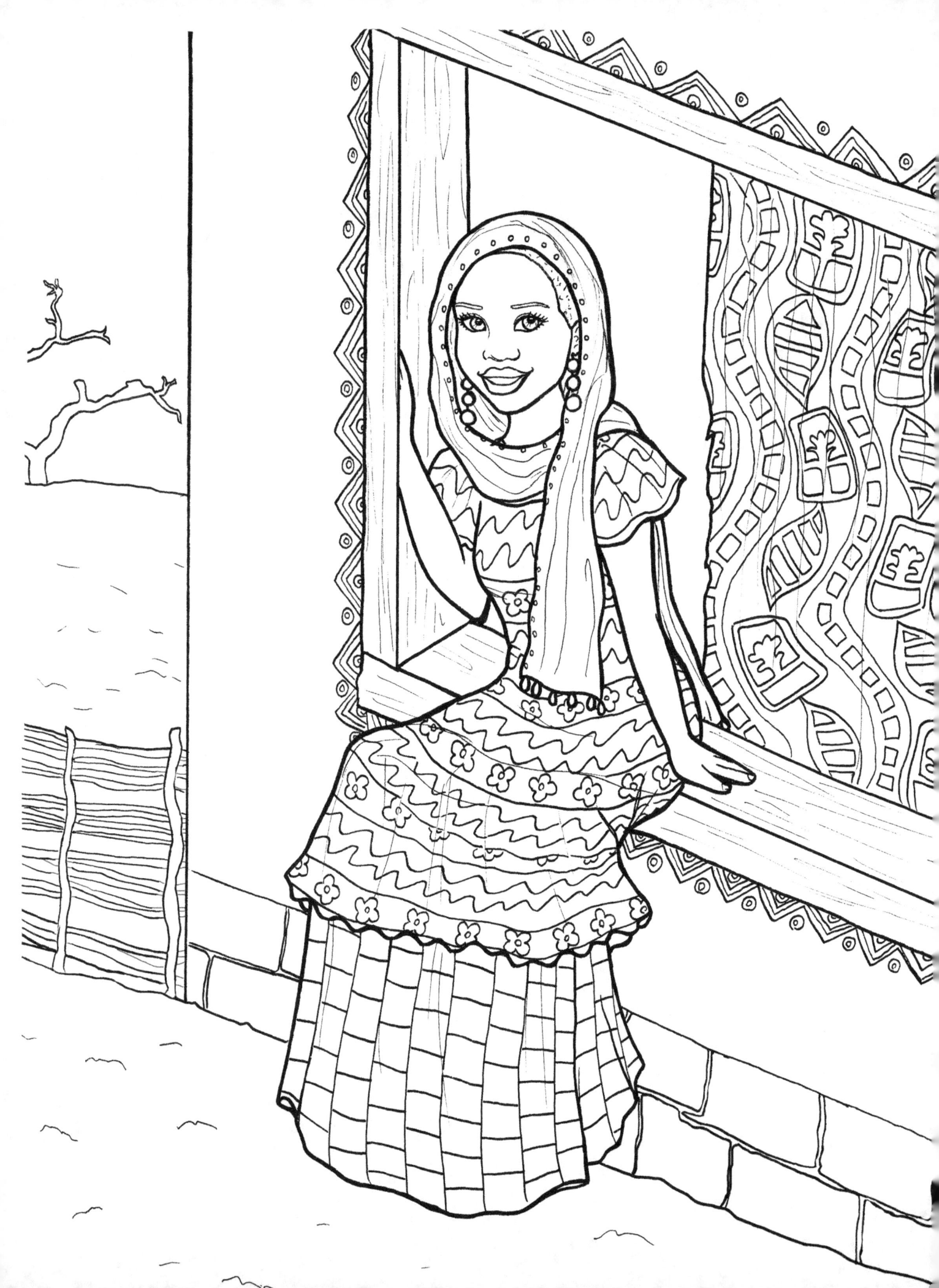

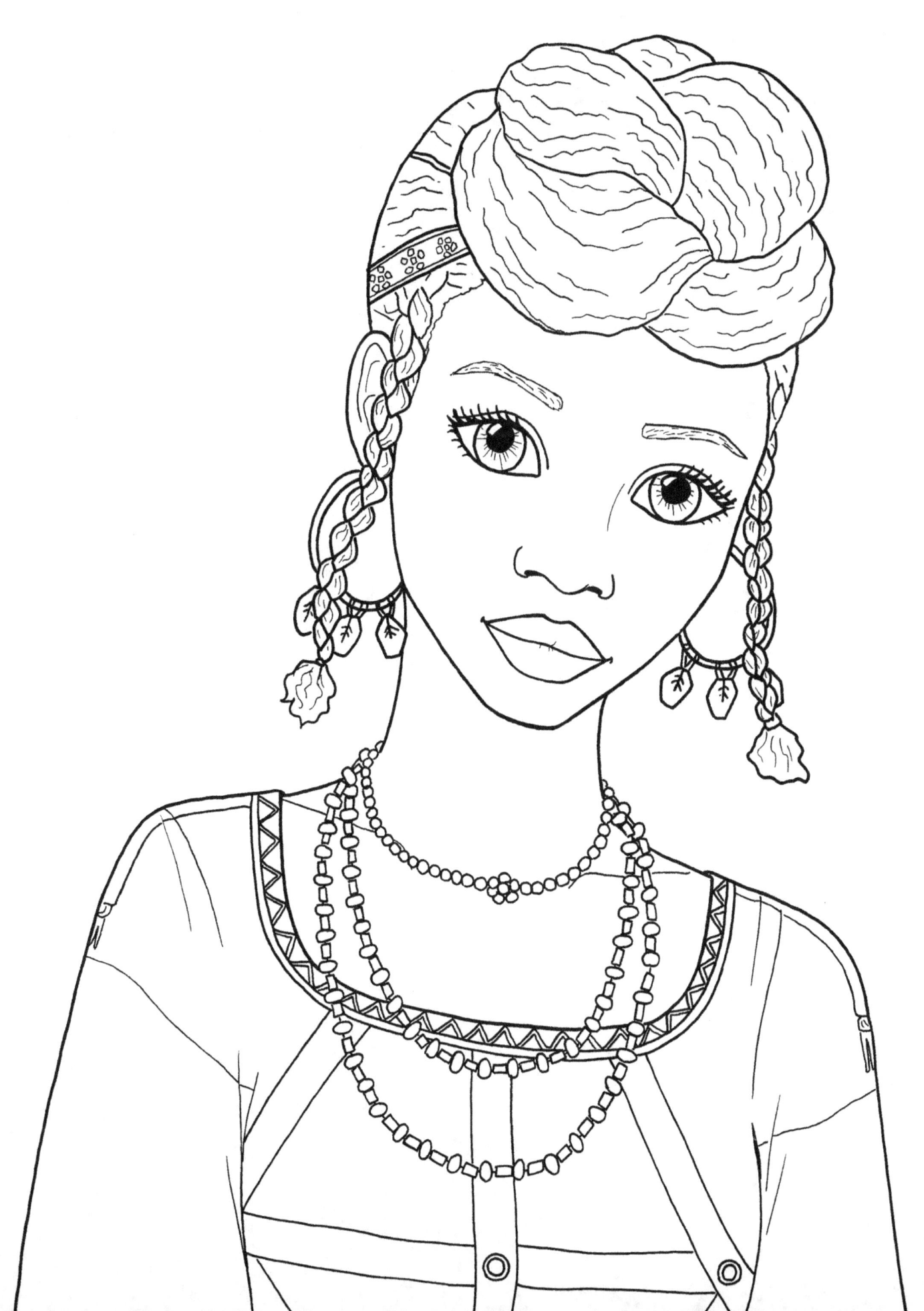

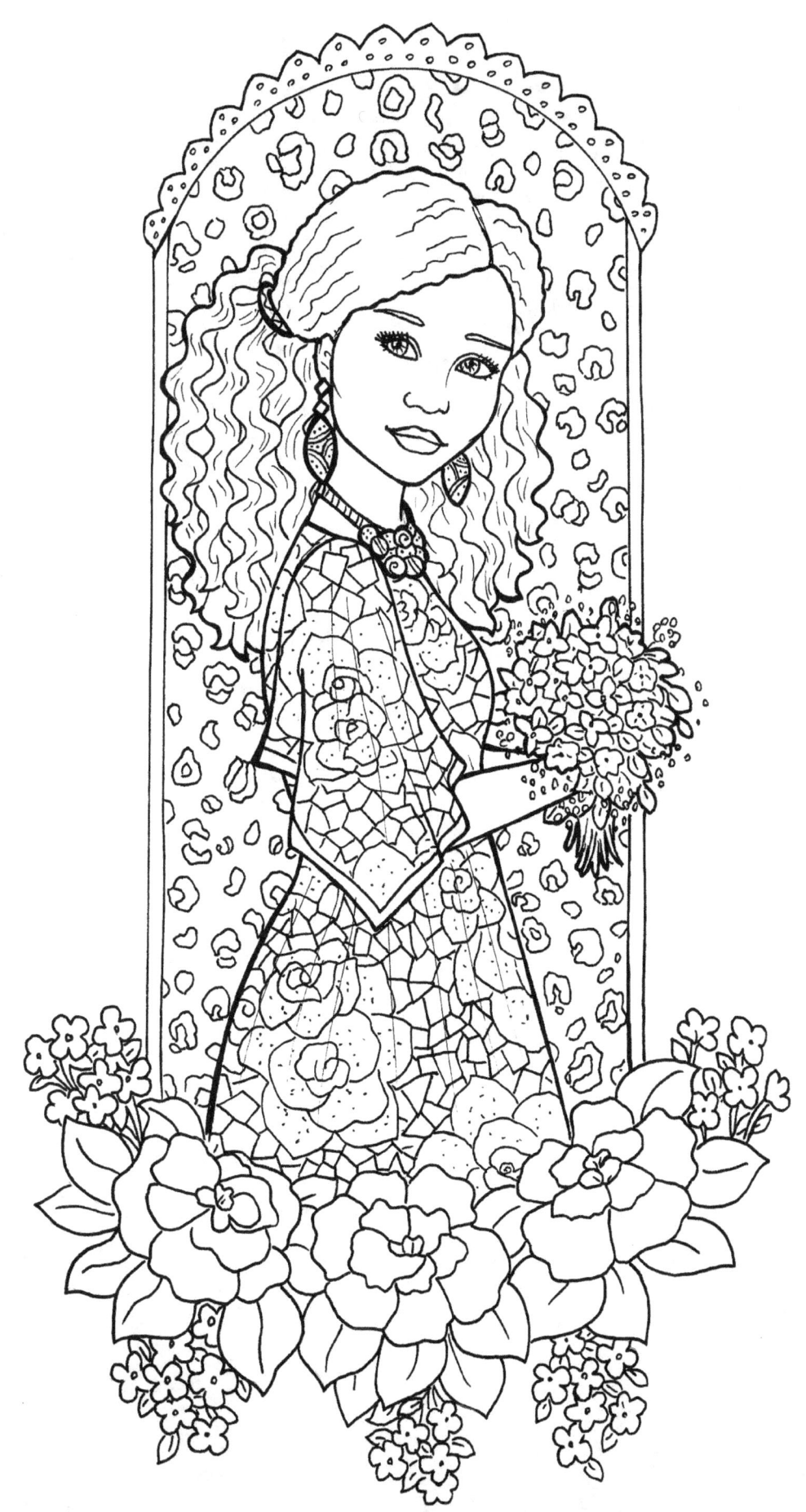

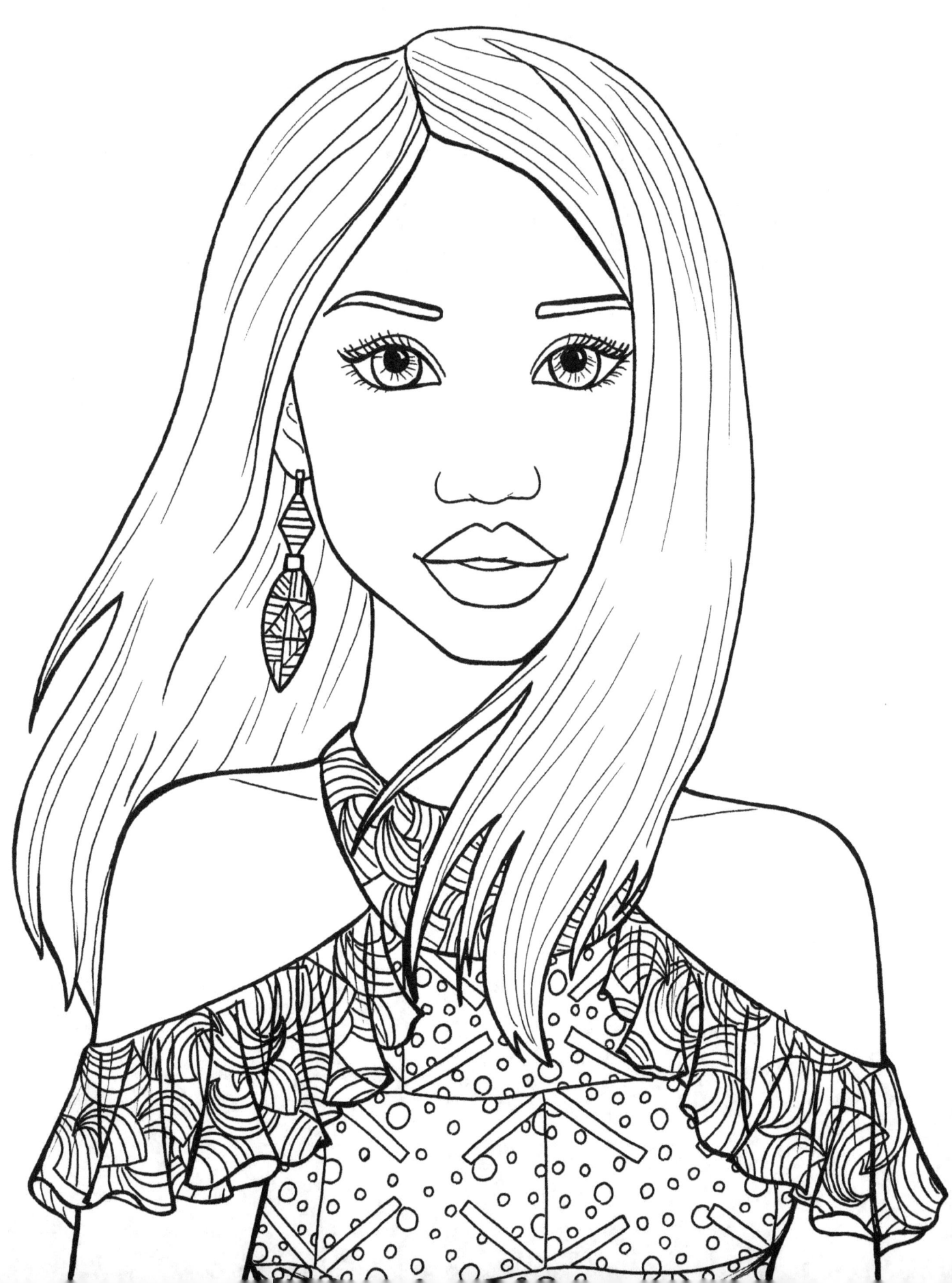

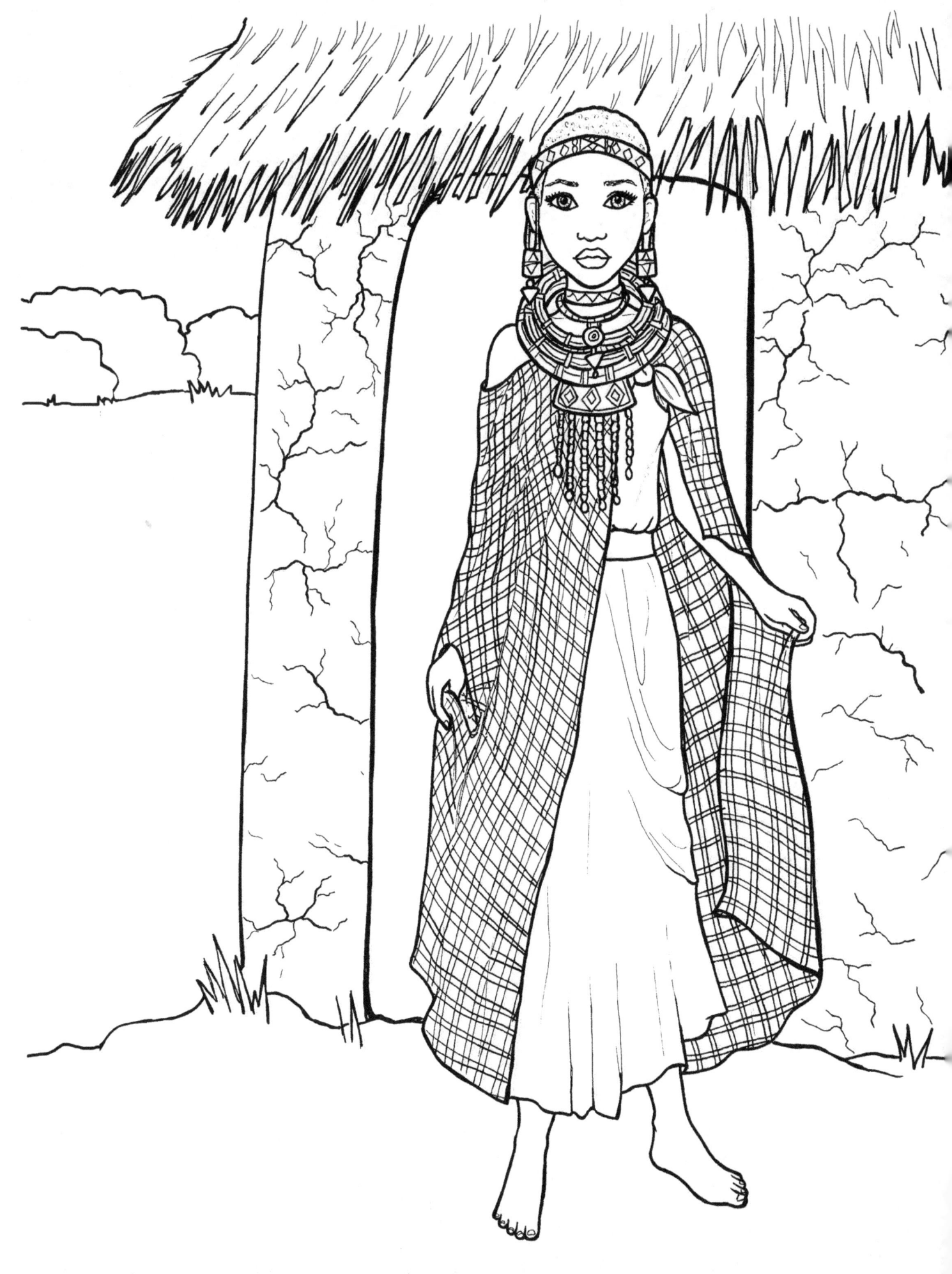

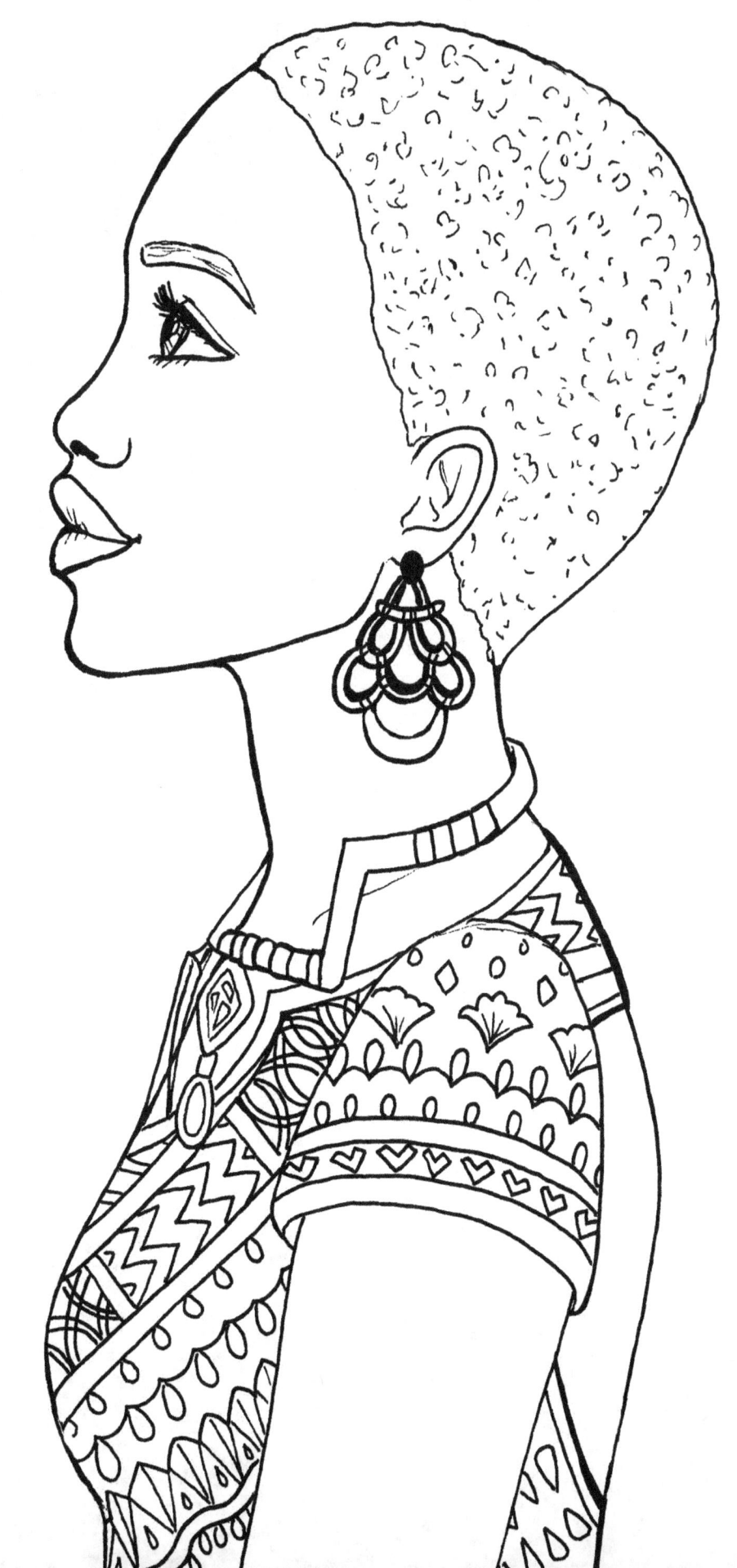

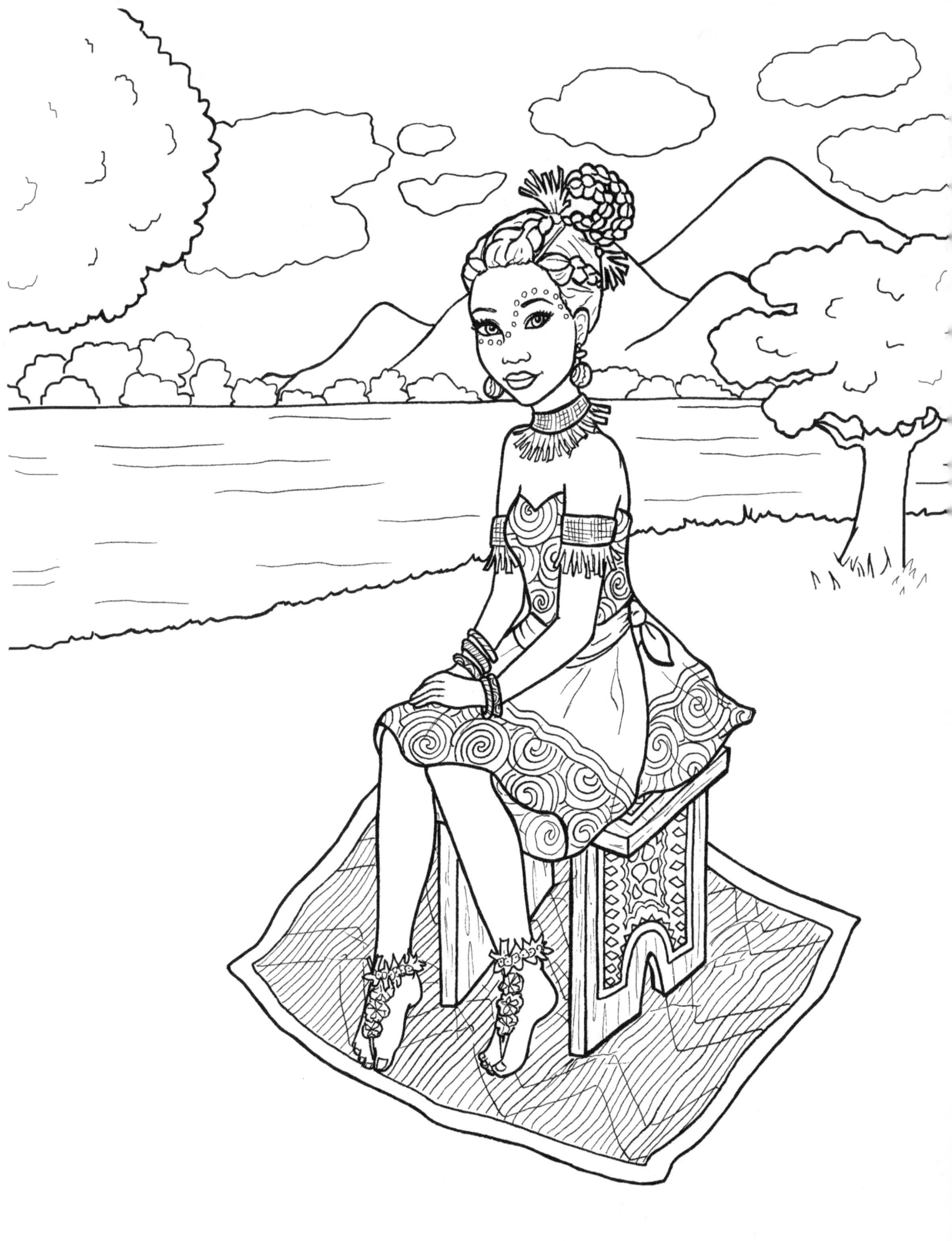

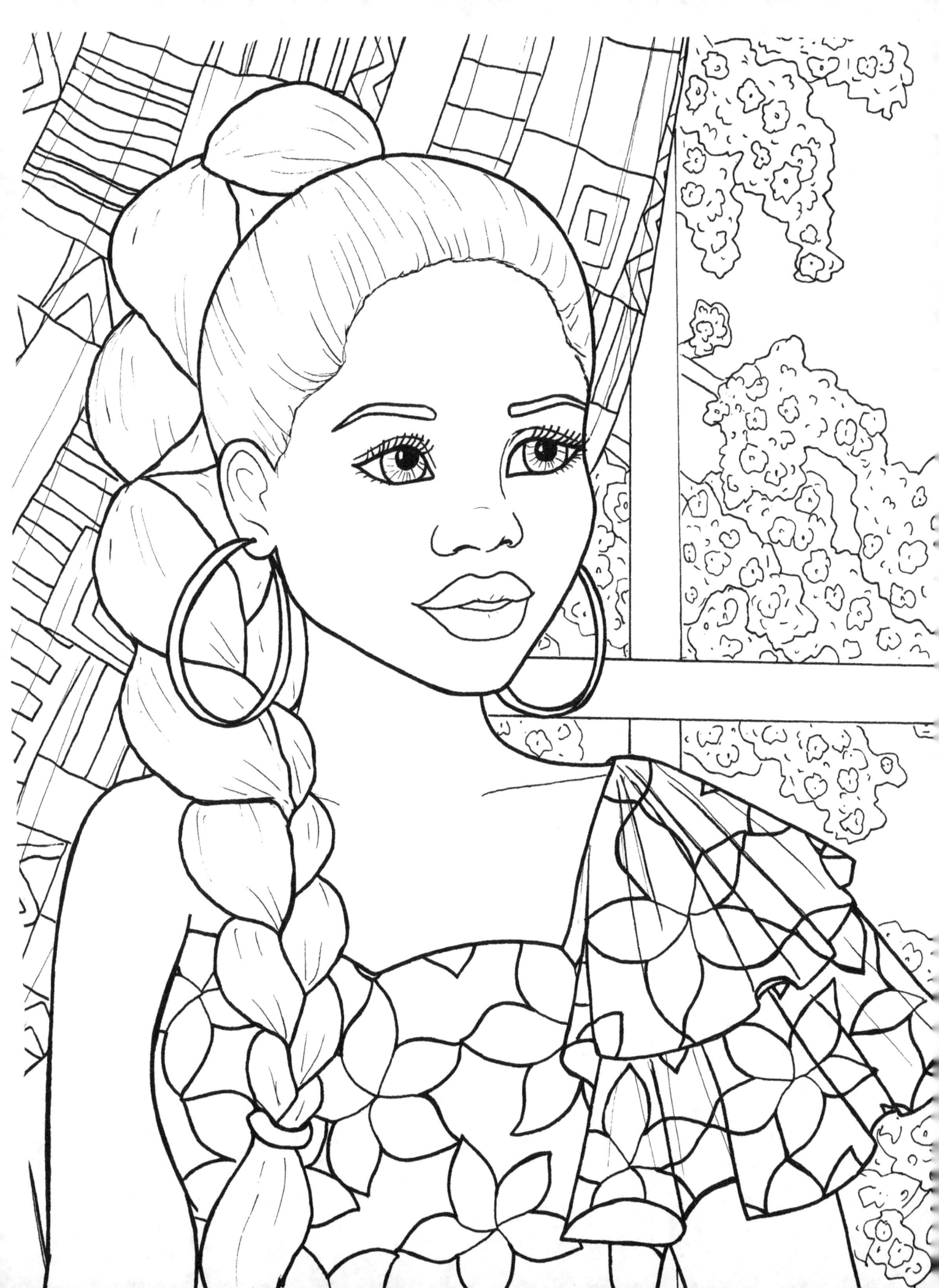

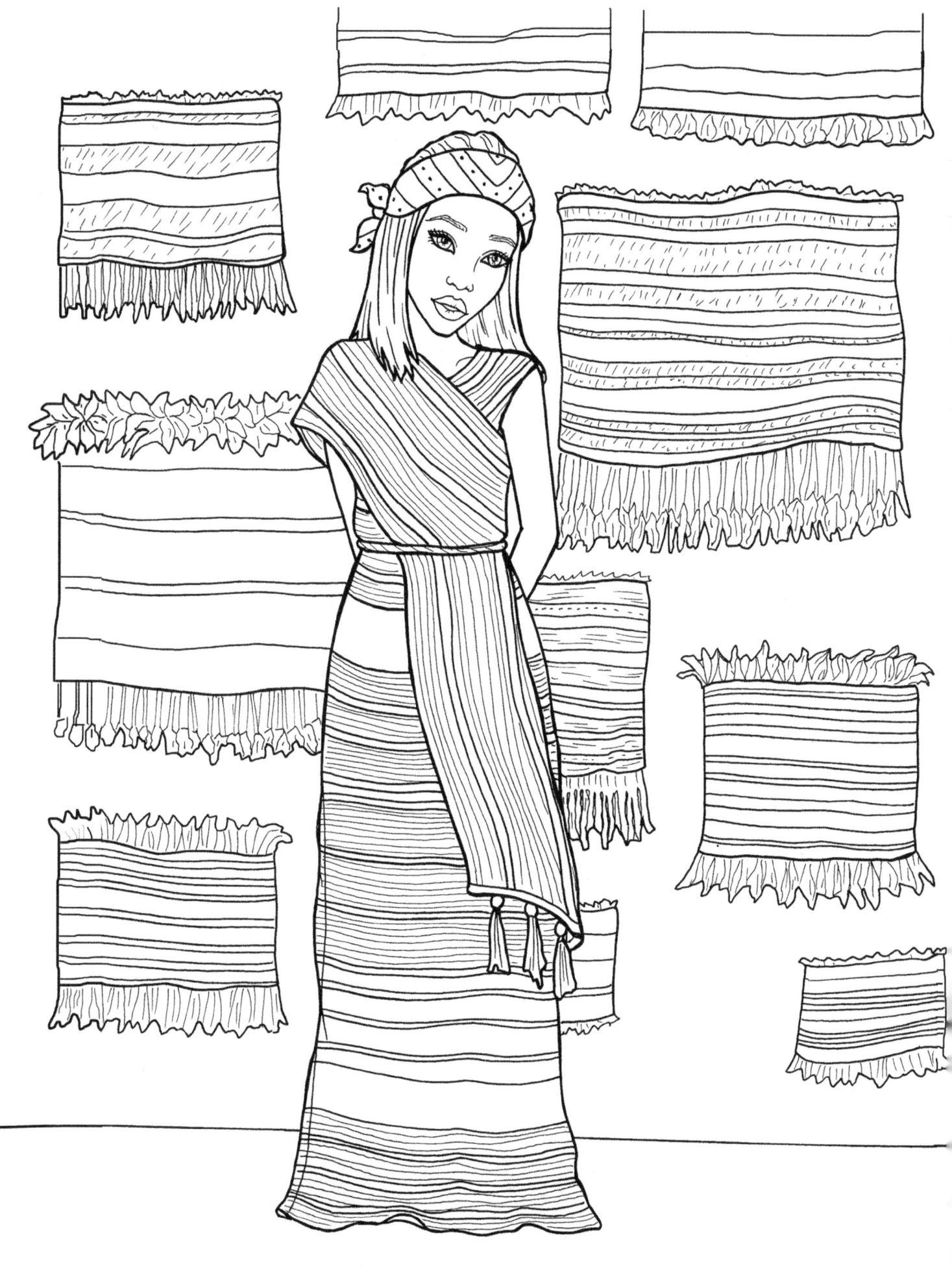

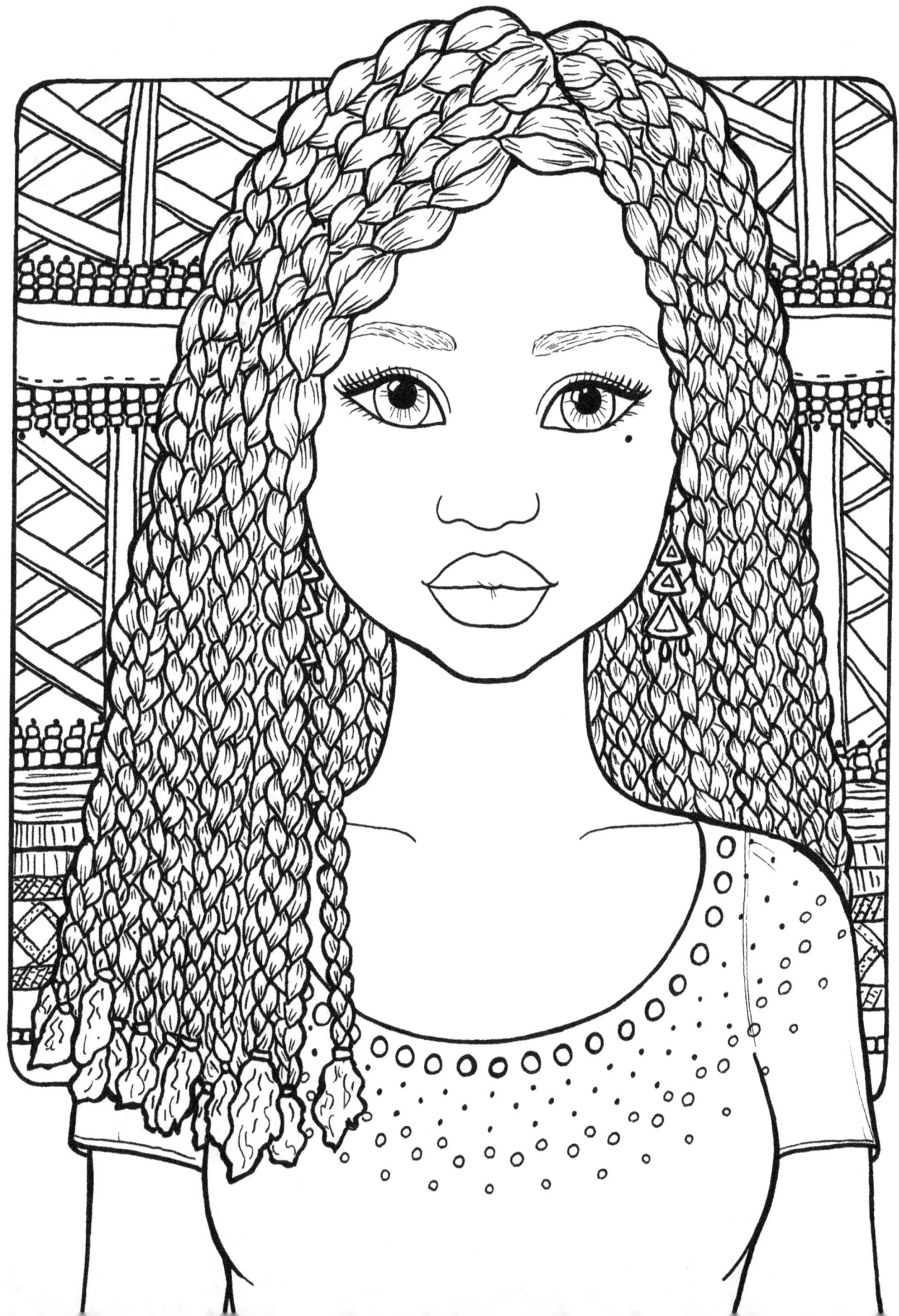

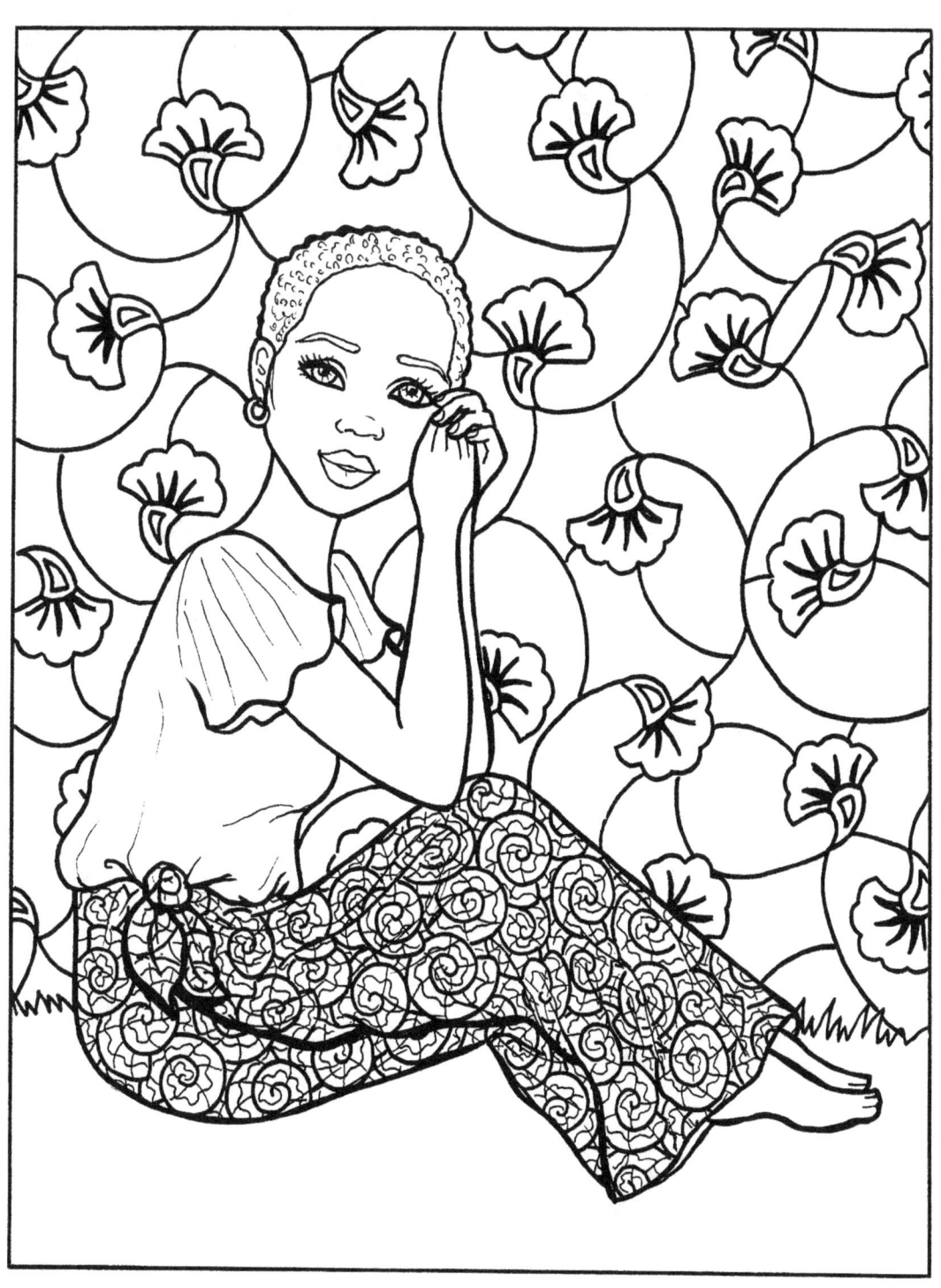

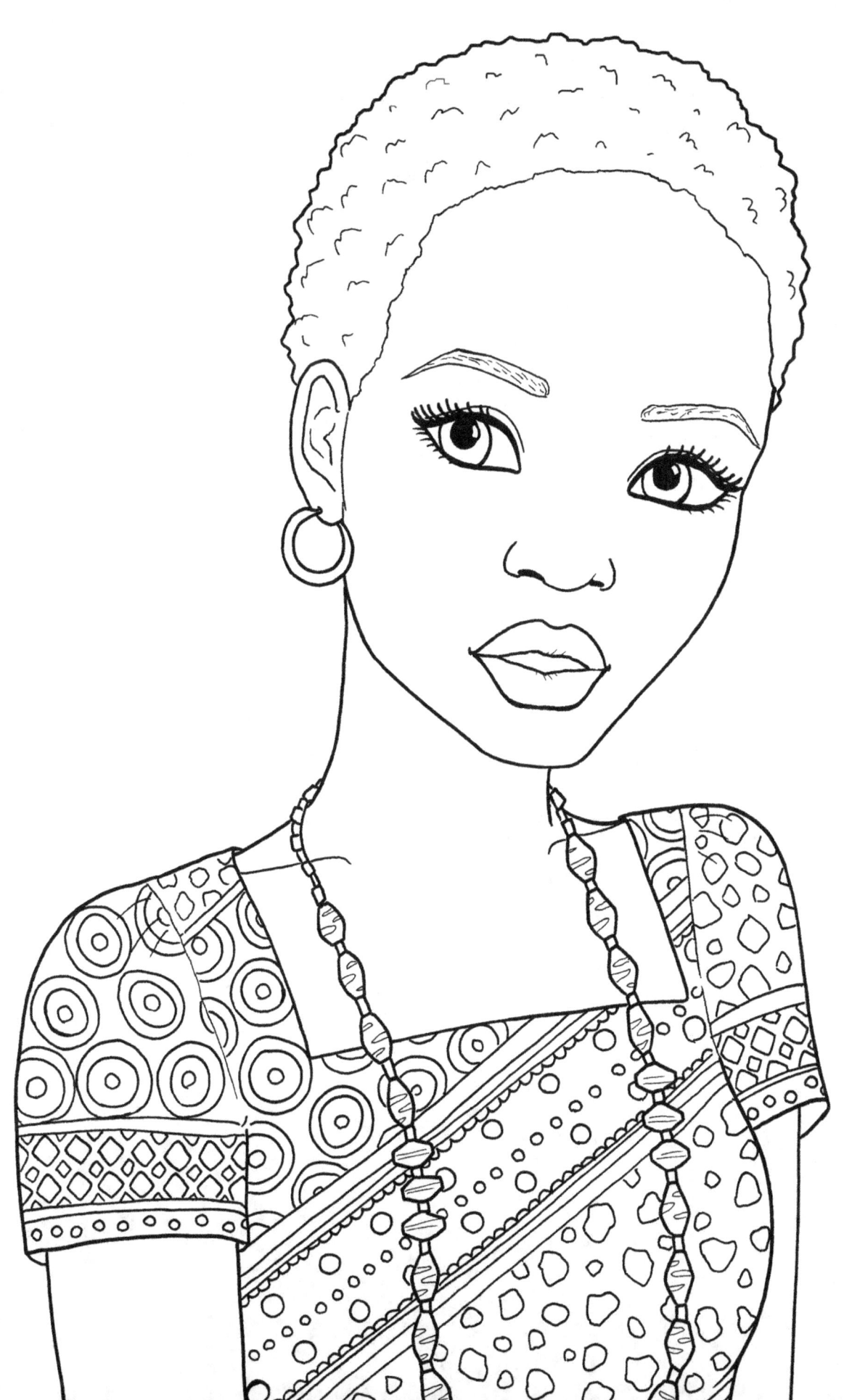

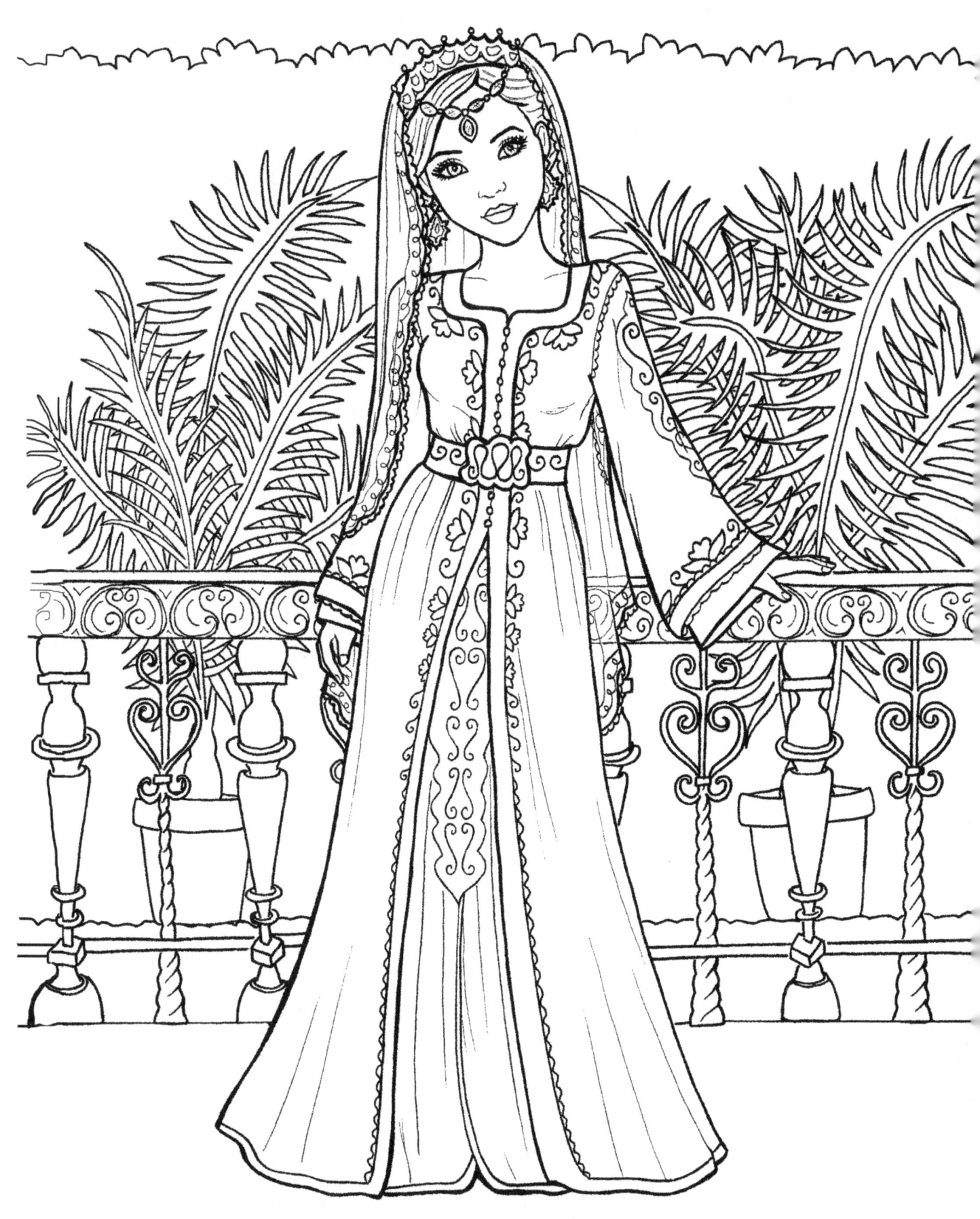

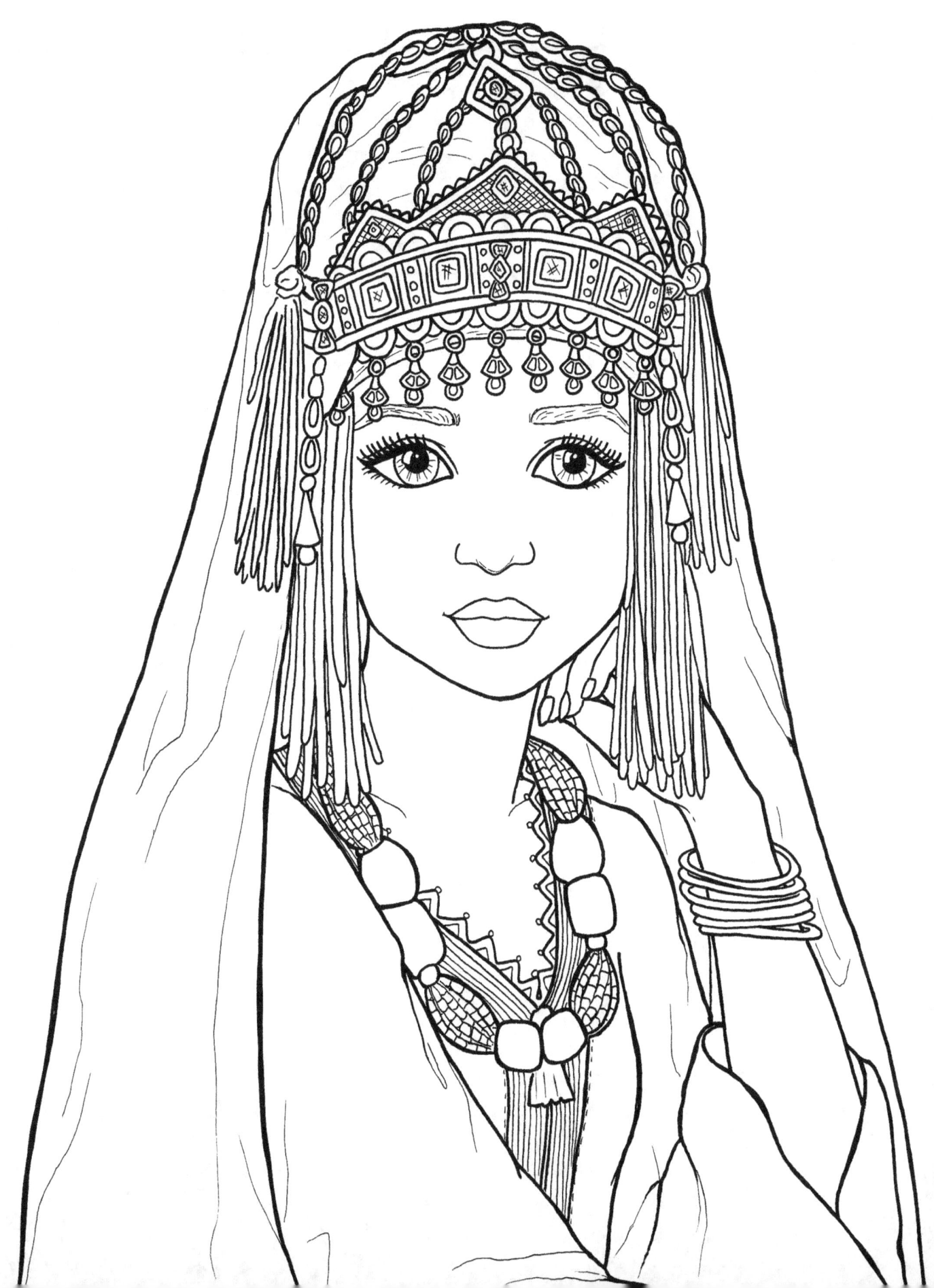

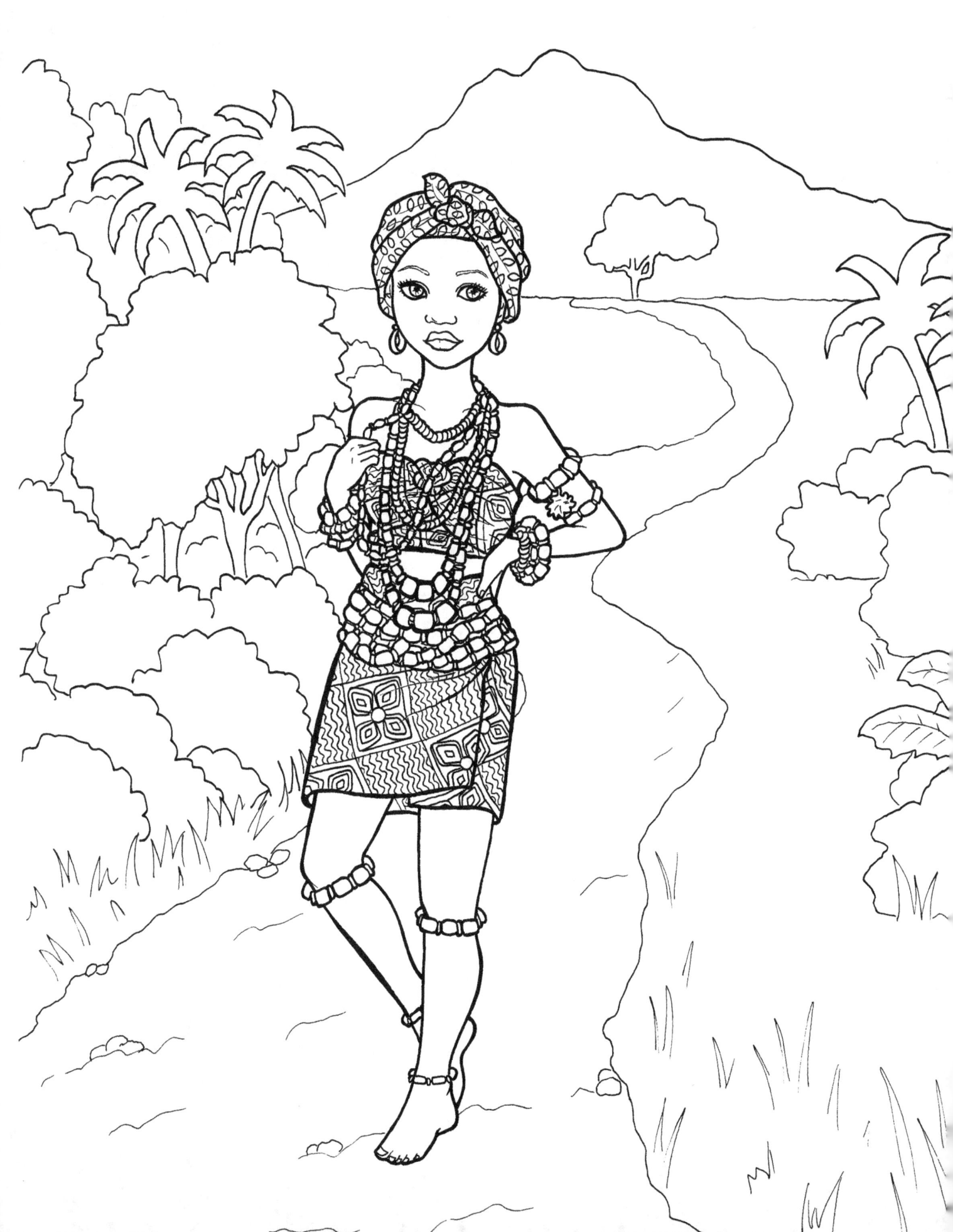

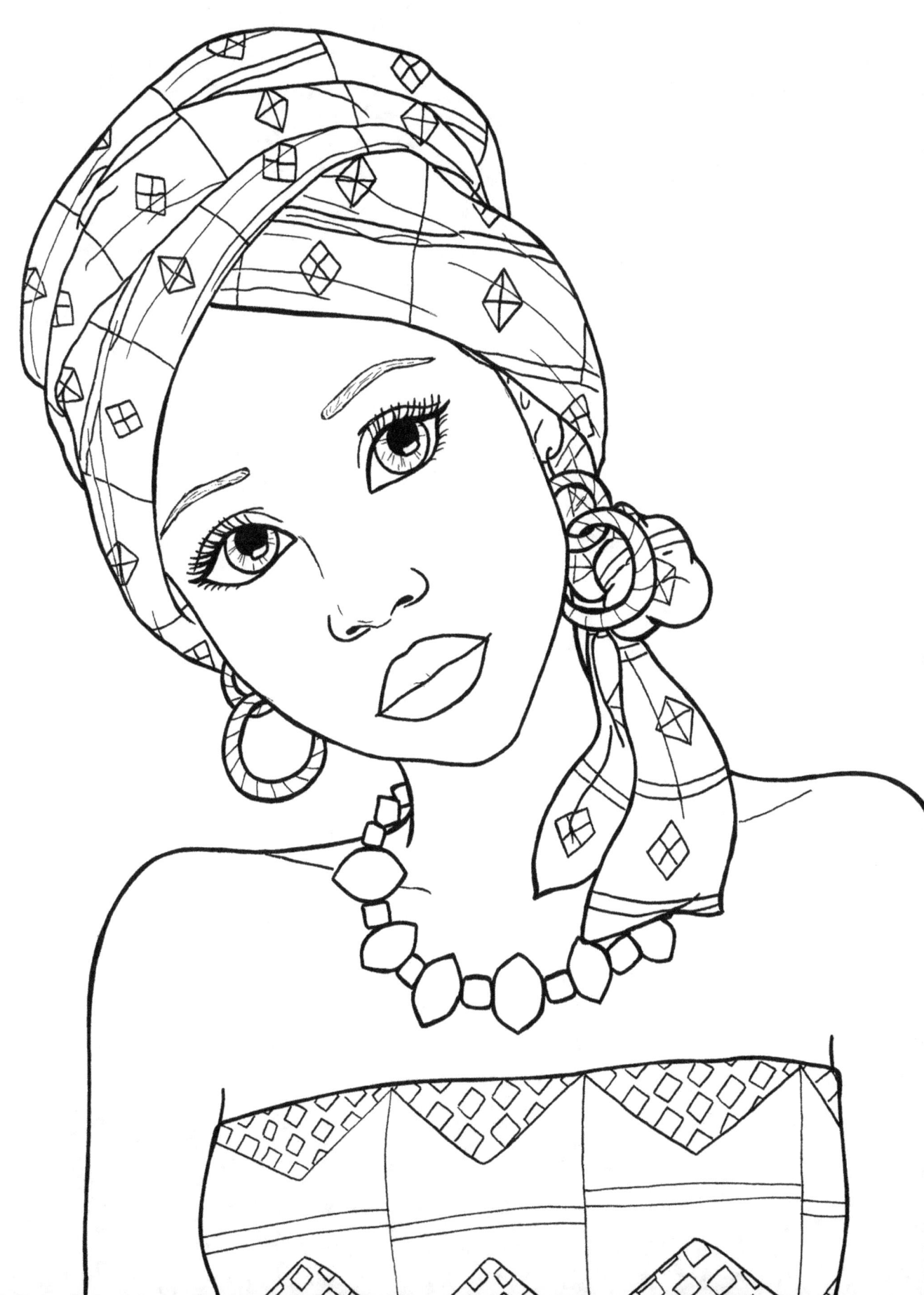

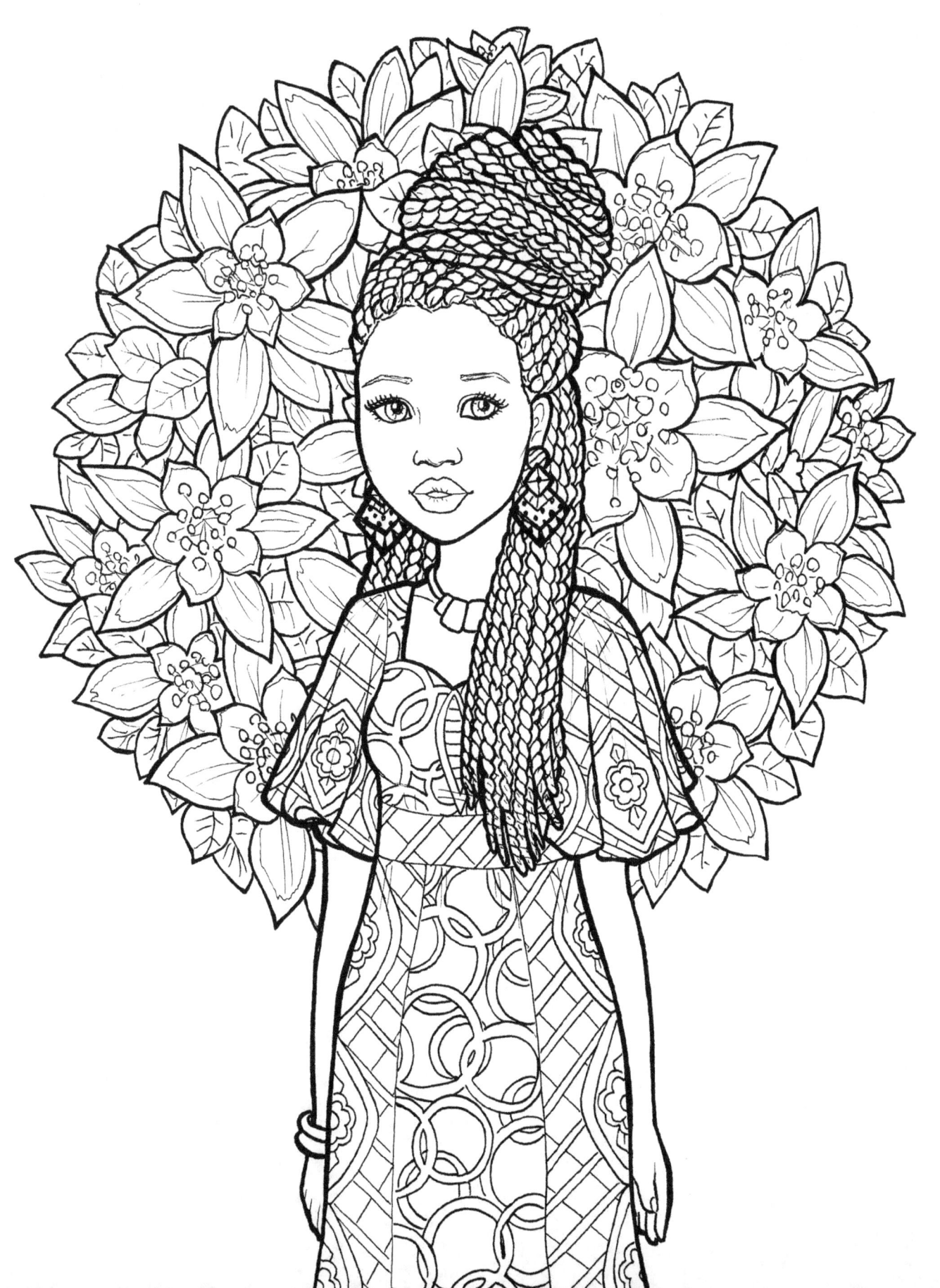

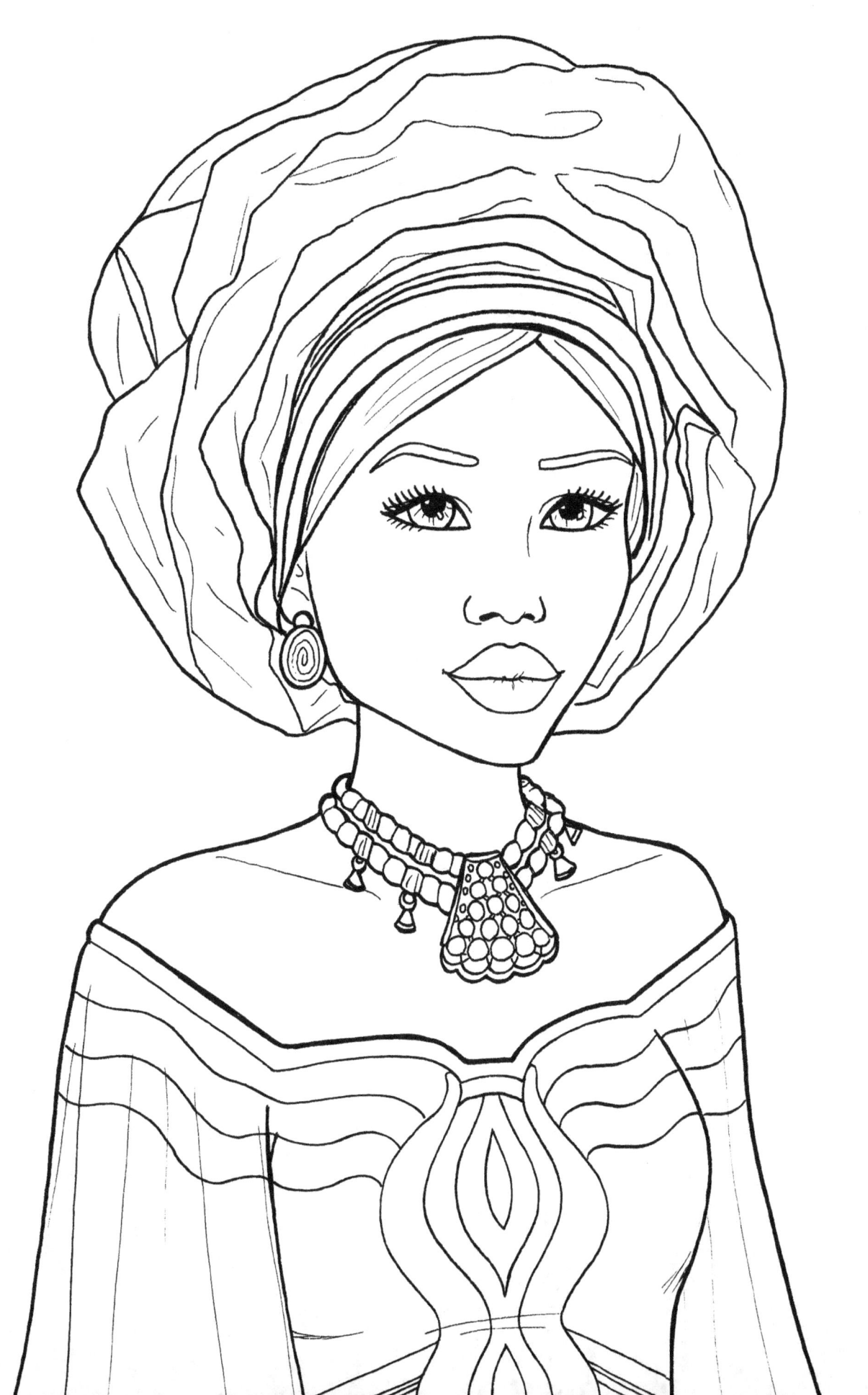

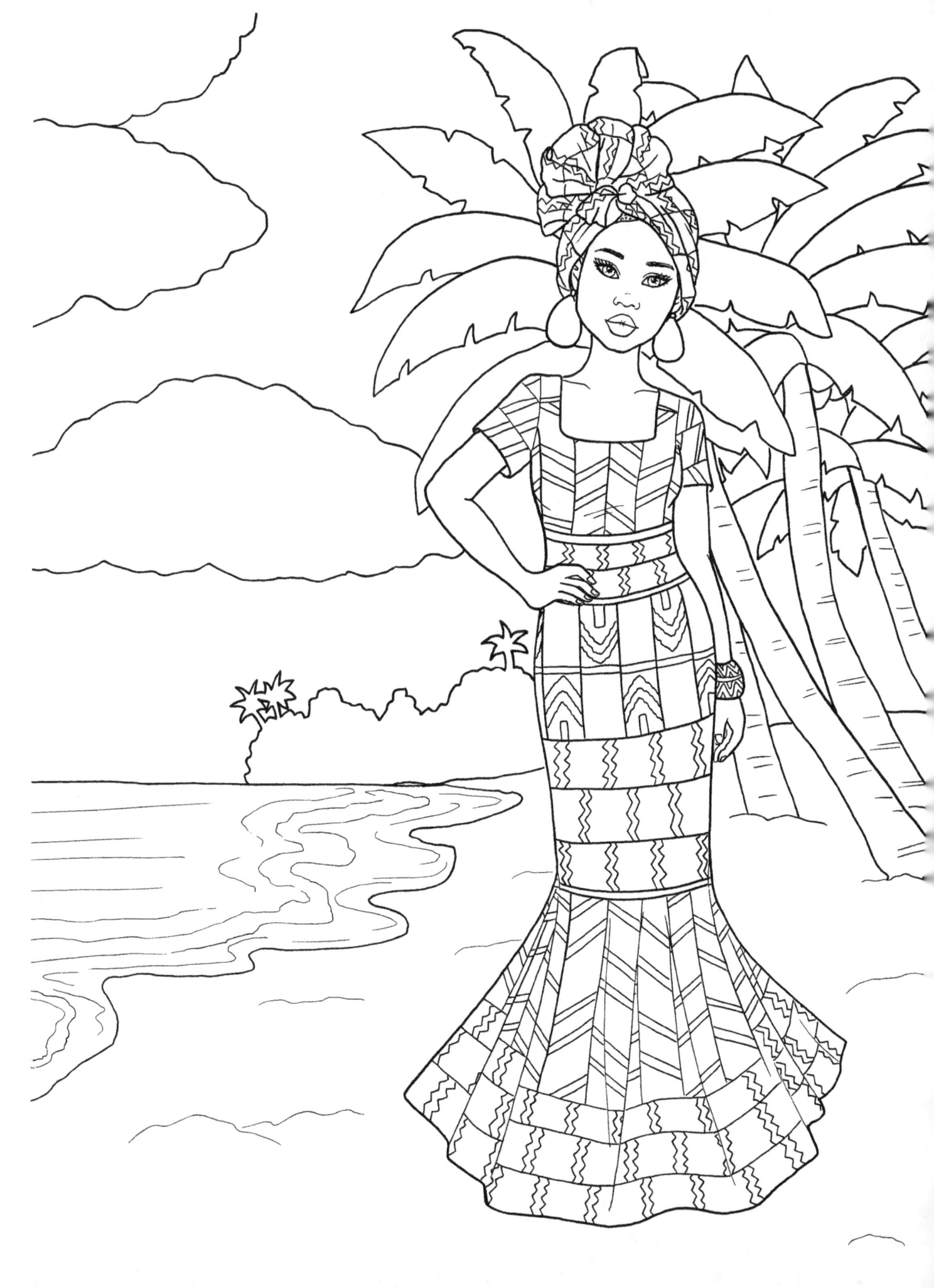

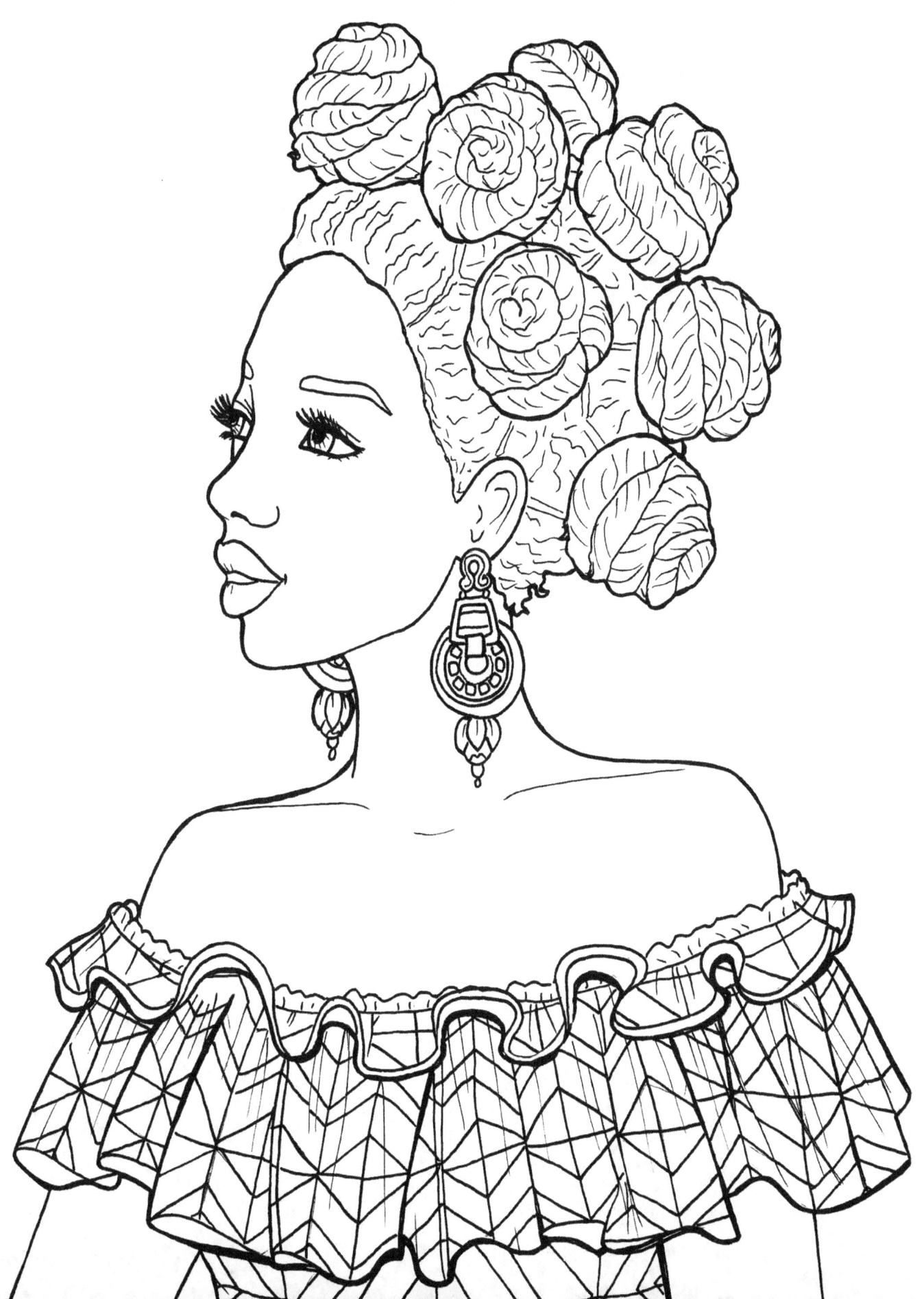

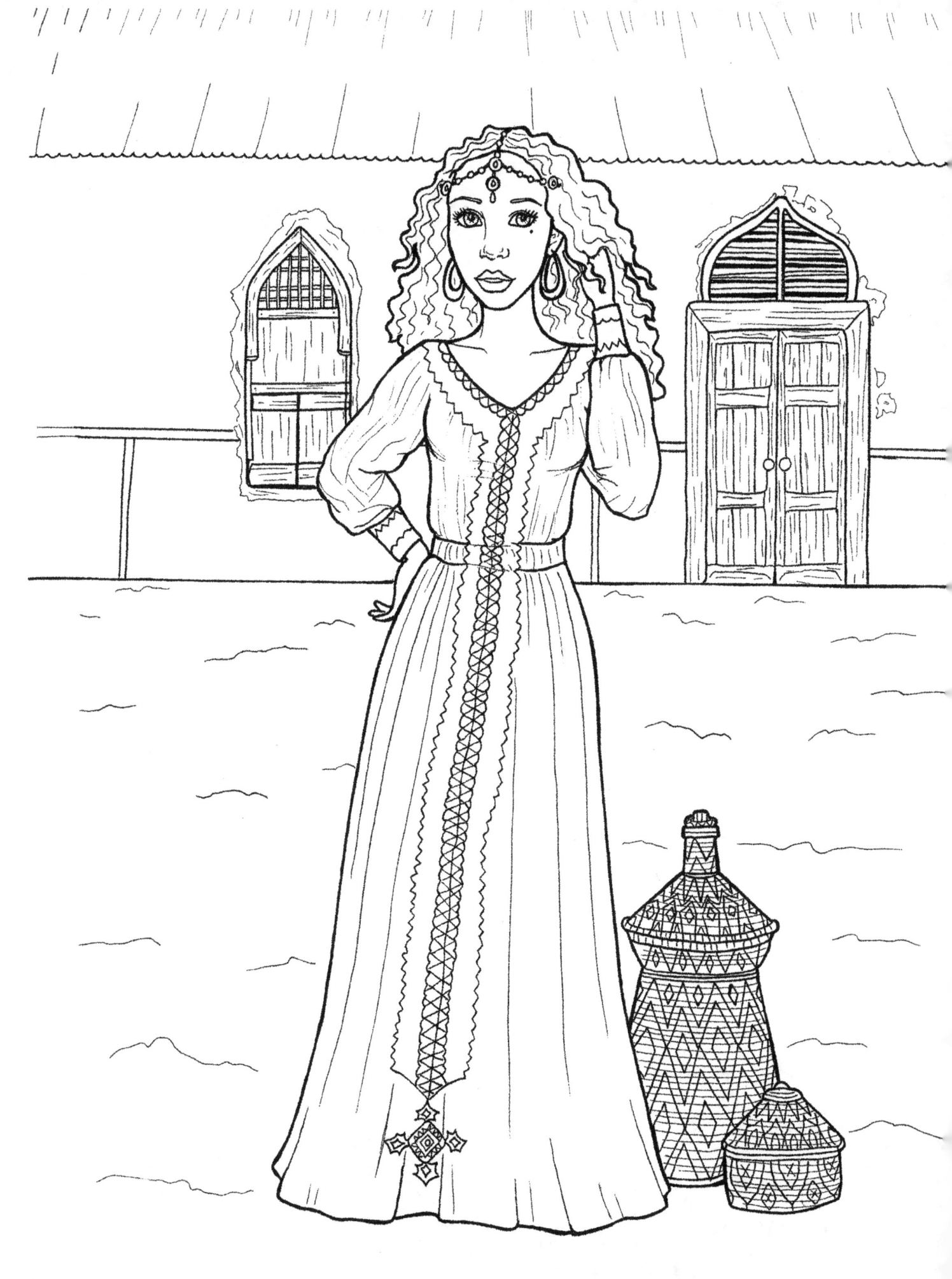

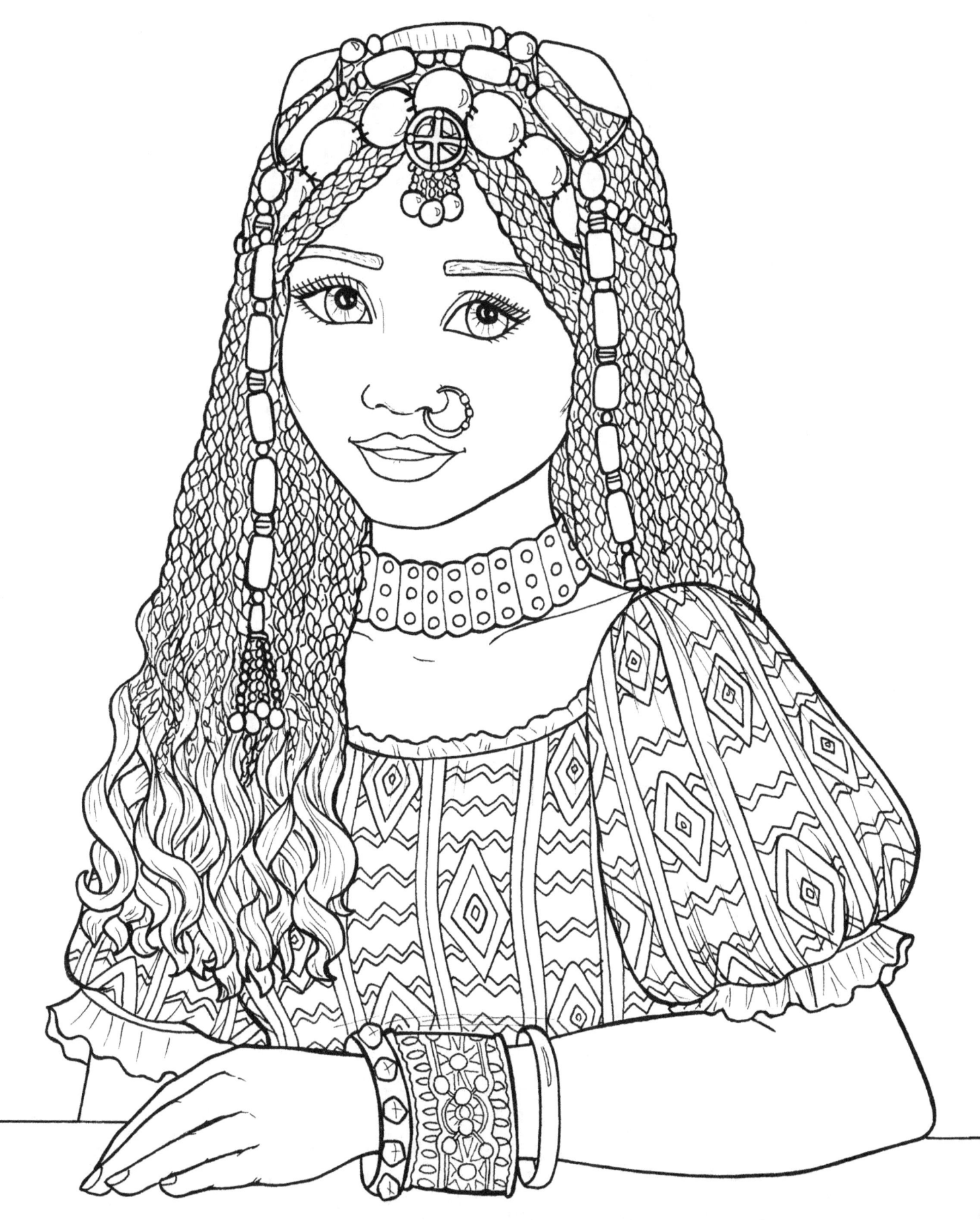

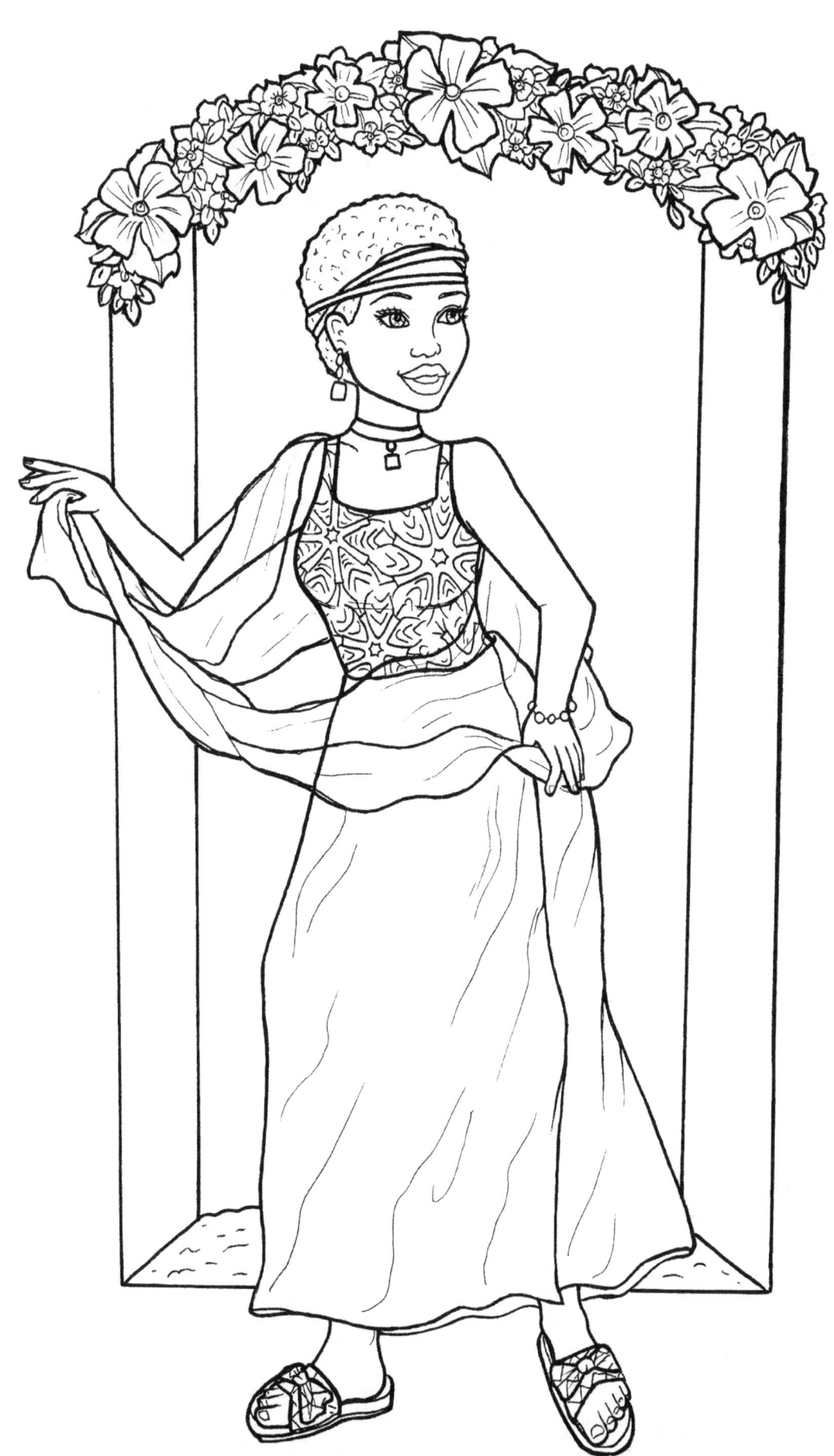

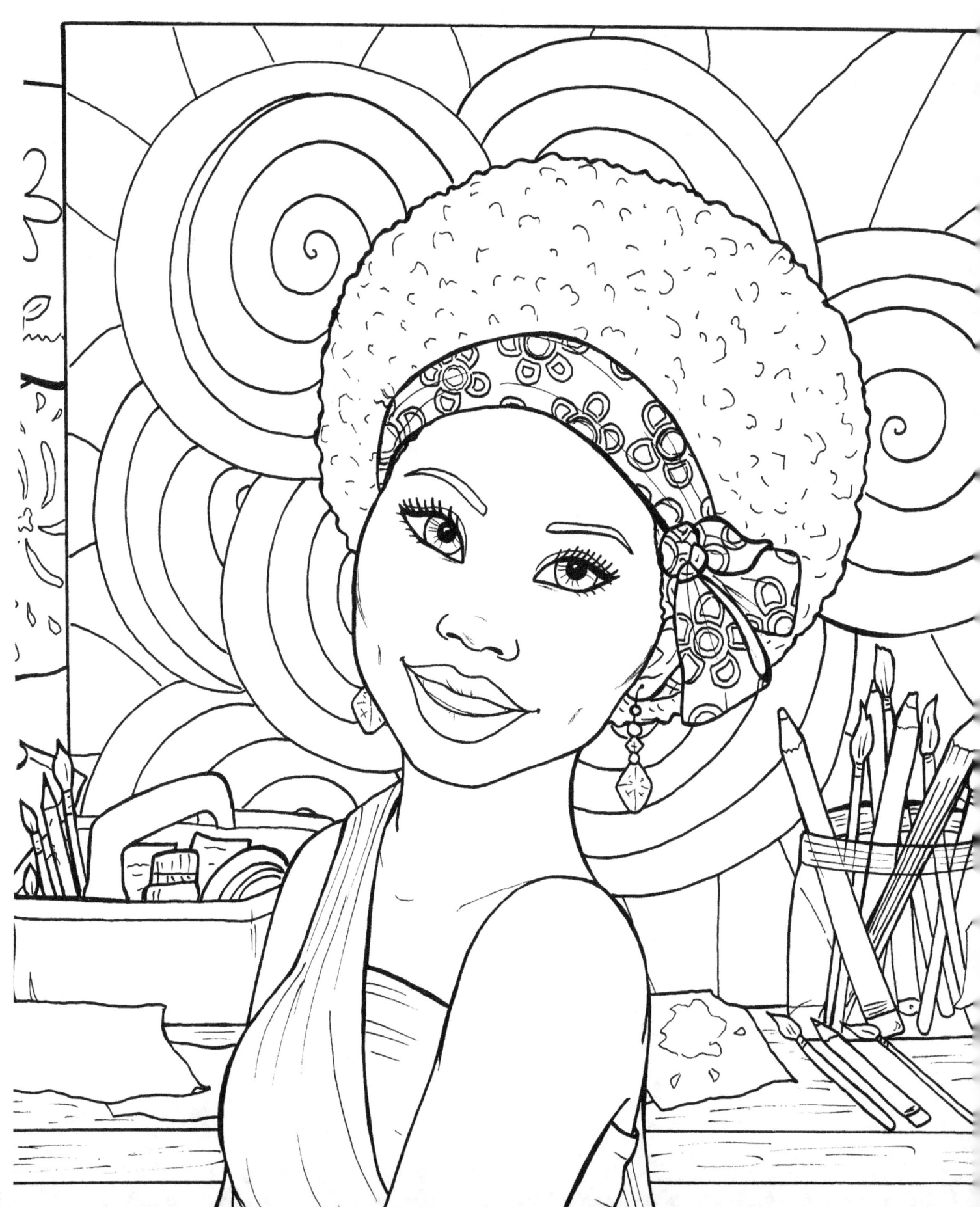

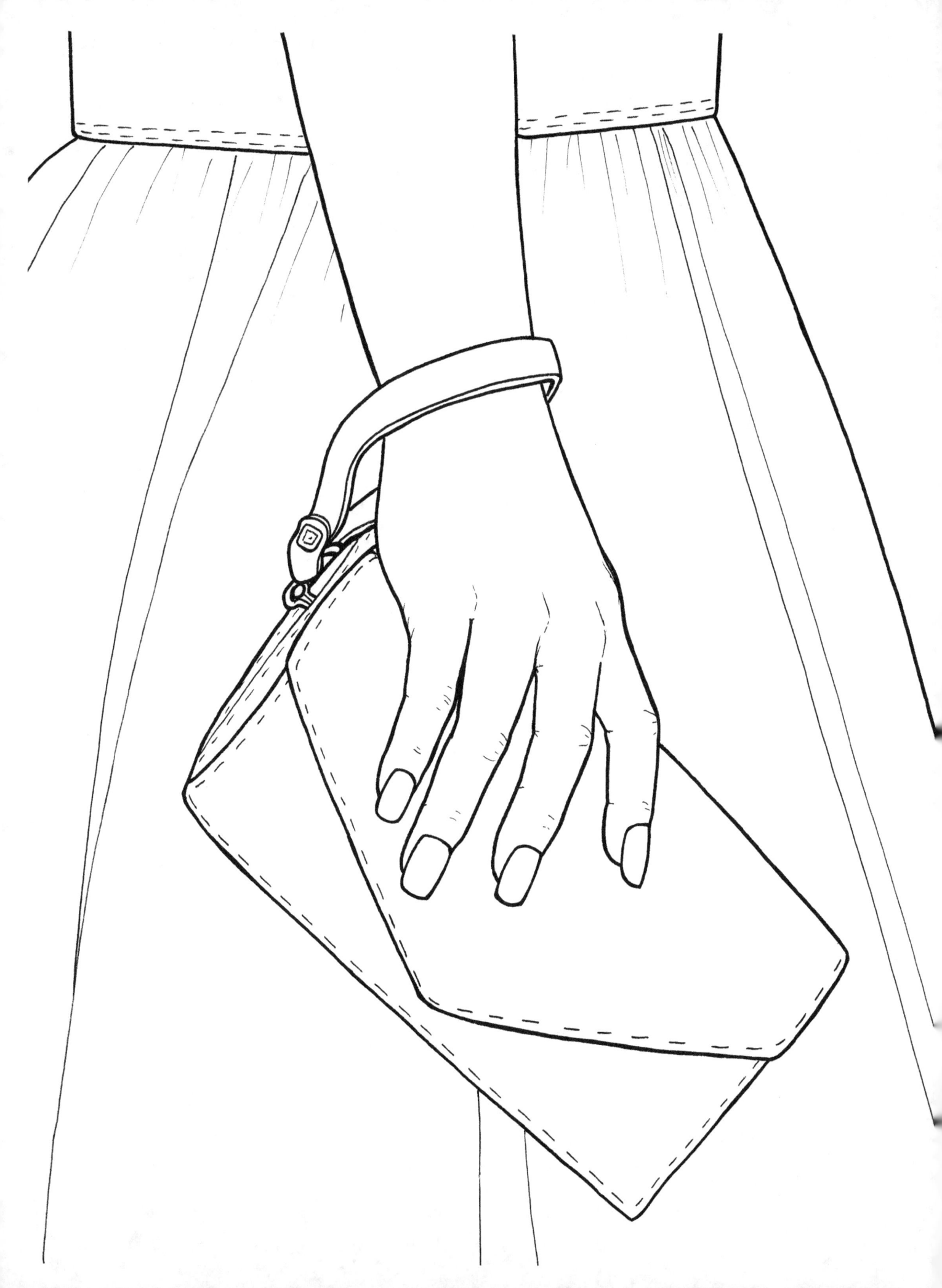

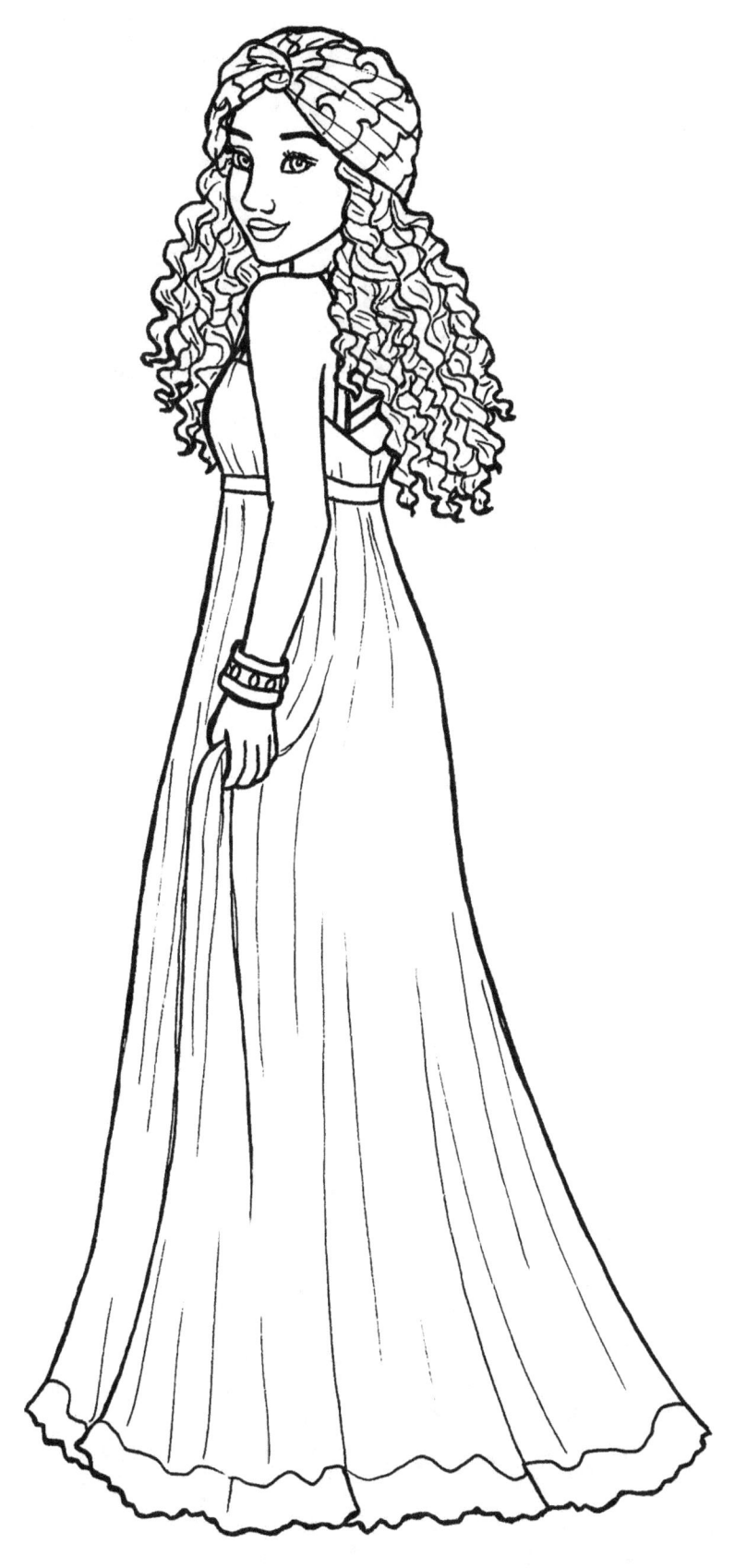

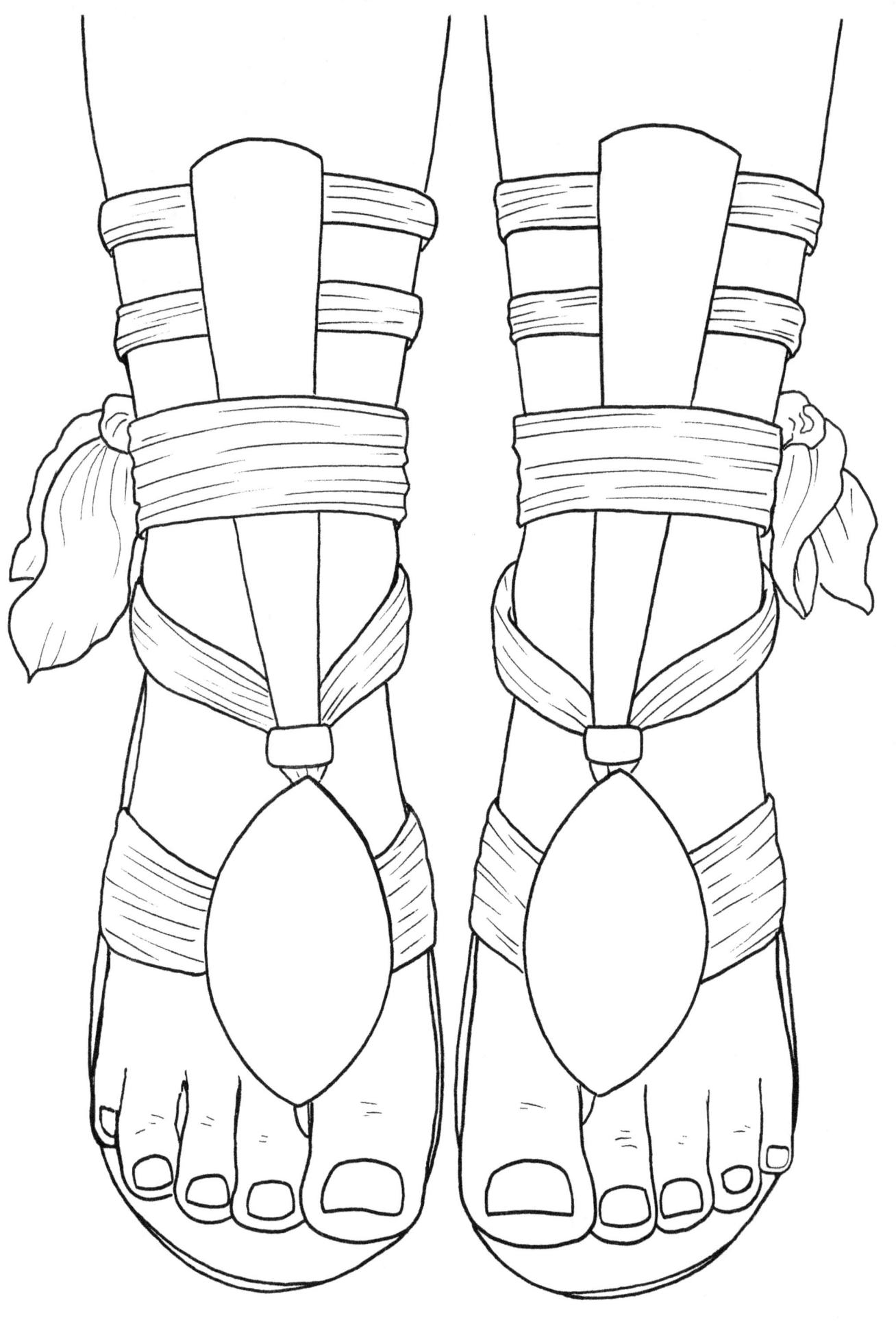

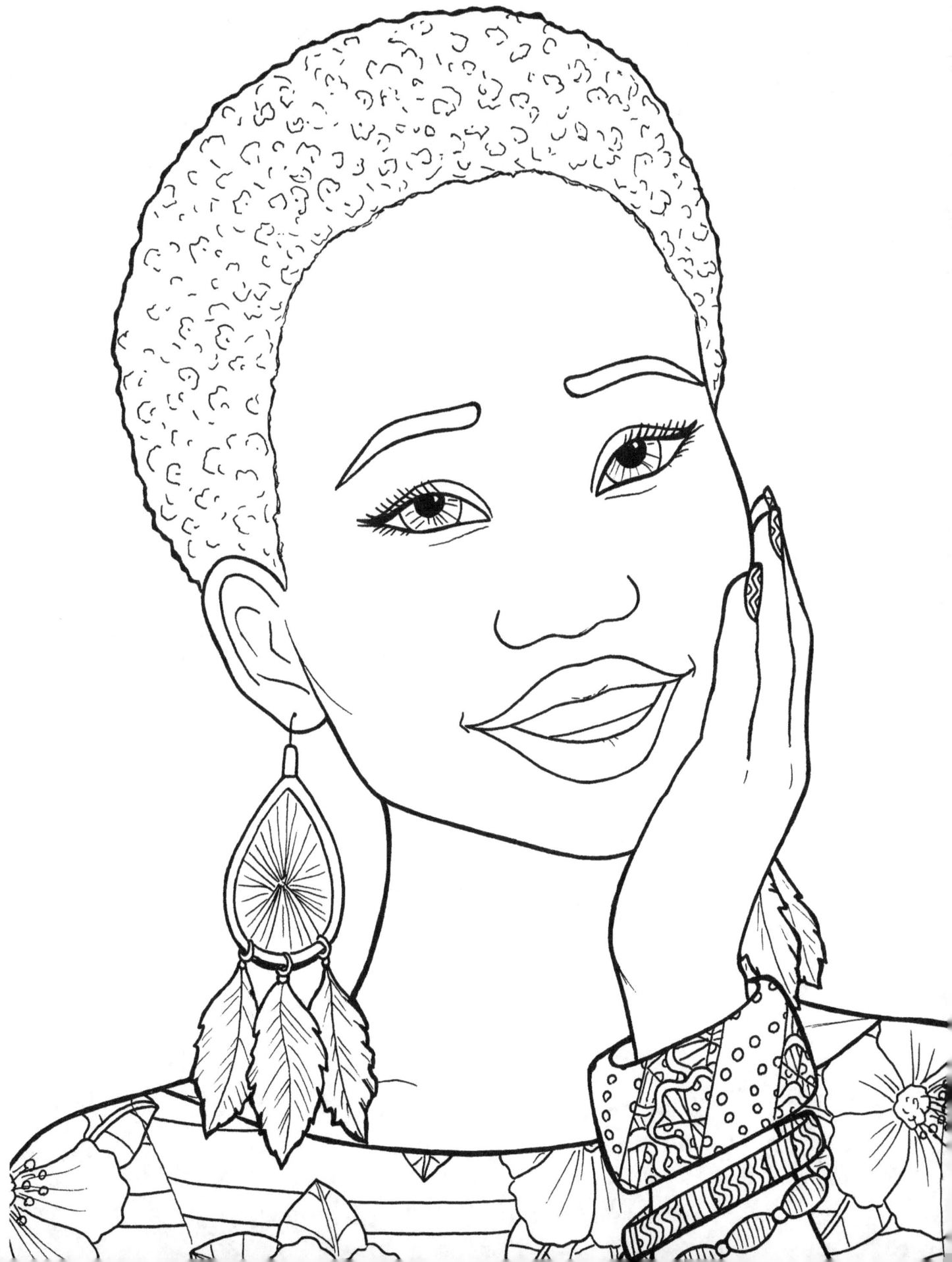

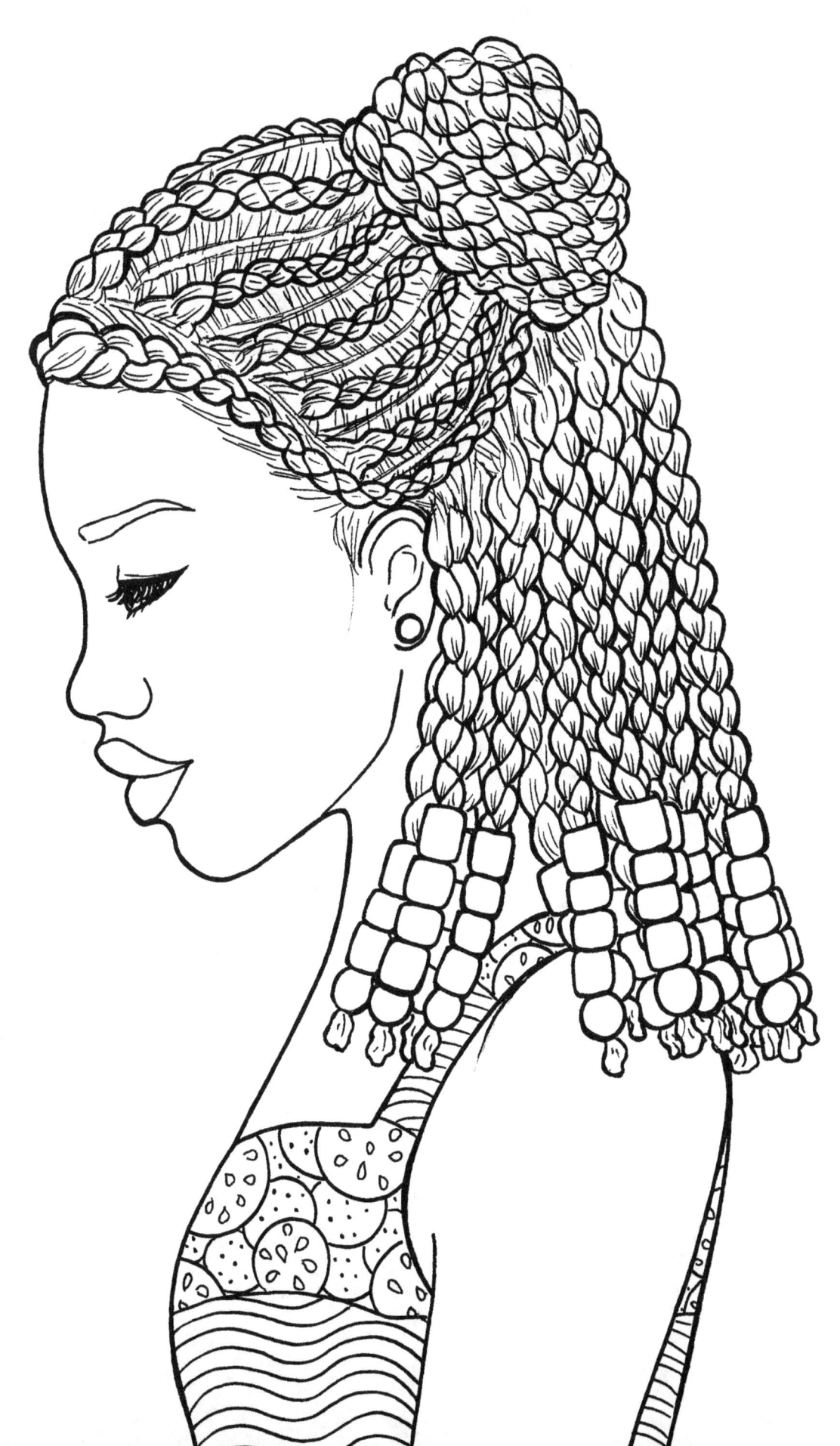

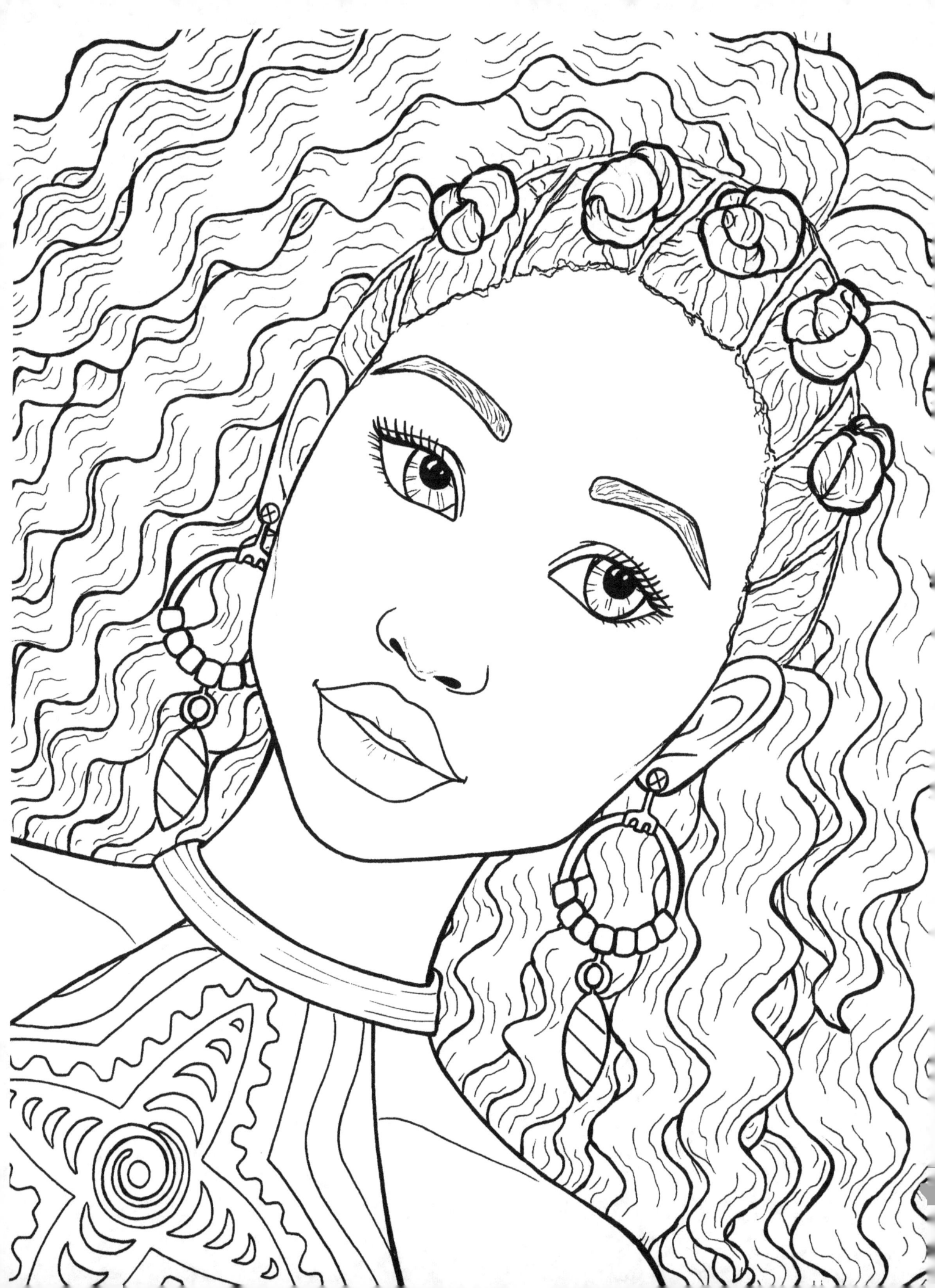

Ready for your next coloring journey? Check out my other book, Nature Inspired Fashions, at Amazon.com.

You can also find a variety of printable coloring pages in my online shop:

www.colorbyculture.com

NATURE INSPIRED
FASHIONS

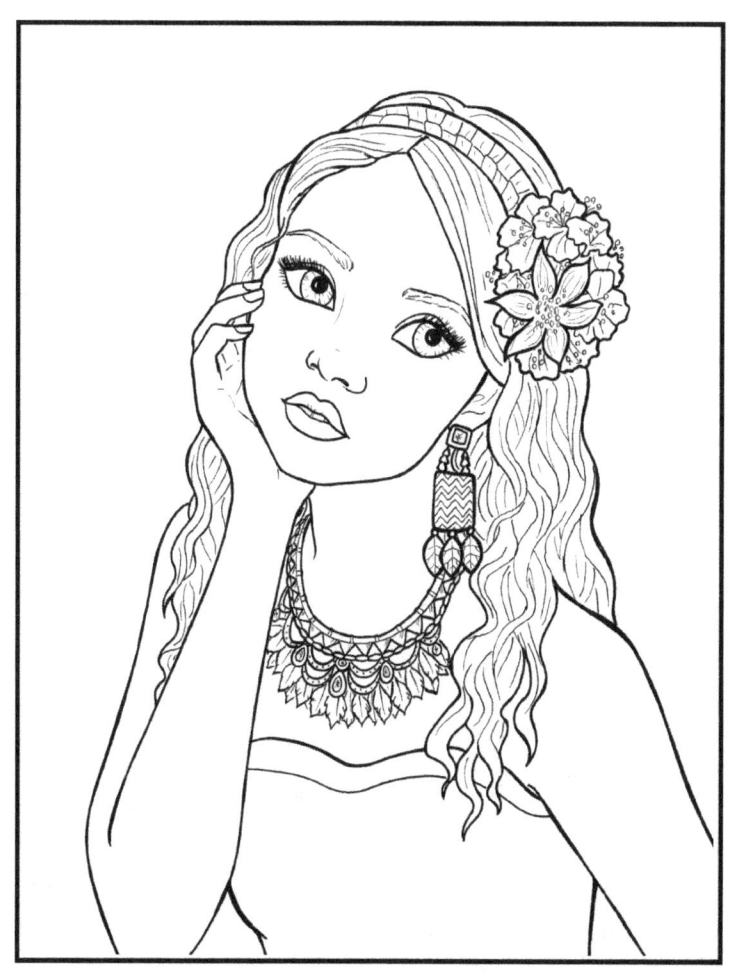